TASTE
& SEE

TASTE & SEE

EXPERIENCING THE STORIES OF ADVENT AND CHRISTMAS

JAN JOHNSON

UPPER ROOM BOOKS®
NASHVILLE

Dedicated to
Larry Peacock
Larry Warner
Directors, Friends, Guides

Taste & See: Experiencing the Stories of Advent and Christmas
Copyright © 2014 by Jan Johnson
All rights reserved.

Upper Room Books® website: books.upperroom.org

Unless otherwise noted, scripture quotations are from the New Revised Standard Version Bible, copyright © 1989 National Council of the Churches of Christ in the United States of America. Used by permission. All rights reserved.

Scripture quotations noted NIV are from the Holy Bible, New International Version®, NIV®. Copyright 1973, 1978, 1984, 2011 by Biblica, Inc.™ Used by permission of Zondervan. All rights reserved worldwide. www.zondervan.com.

Scripture quotations noted KJV are from the King James Version of the Holy Bible.

Scripture quotations noted The Message are from *THE MESSAGE*. Copyright © 1993, 1994, 1995, 1996, 2000, 2001, 2002. Used by permission of NavPress Publishing Group.

At the time of publication all website references in this book were valid. However, due to the fluid nature of the internet some addresses may have changed or the content may not longer be relevant.

Cover design: Nelson Kane
Interior design: PerfecType, Nashville, TN

Library of Congress Cataloging-in-Publication Data

Johnson, Jan
  Taste and see: experiencing the stories of Advent and Christmas / Jan Johnson.
      pages cm
  ISBN 978-0-8358-1354-9 (print) — ISBN 978-0-8358-1355-6 (mobi) — ISBN 978-0-8358-1356-3 (epub)
  1. Bible. Luke I-II—Meditations. 2. Bible. Matthew I, 18-25—Meditations. 3. Advent—Meditations. 4. Christmas—Meditations. I. Title.
  BS2595.54.J64 2014
      242'.33—dc23   2014007540
Printed in the United States of America

CONTENTS

Week 3: Experiencing Joseph's Challenge

Week 4: Experiencing the Birth of Christ

*Possible Christmas Eve or Christmas Day Meditation

Post–Advent: Experiencing the Journey to Safety (Matthew 2:13-23)

INTRODUCTION

You probably know well the stories that surround the Christmas events. Maybe you love them or maybe you're a little bored with them, but something makes you want to experience Christ in Christmas in a fuller way.

The focus of our time together will be much more than to remember the Christmas story. We will aim to *experience* the events of Christmas ourselves. This guide invites you to "taste and see," to imagine the tangible elements in the stories and the probable feelings of the characters. Historical and cultural facts provide context and a means of stepping into these events and these lives for a while. While you probably are embarking on this study in order to celebrate Christmas in a meaningful way (and to enjoy fellowship with others if you're doing this with a group), be prepared for God to speak to you in ways that meet deep needs within you.

SOME THINGS TO KEEP IN MIND

A Different Way to Read

In school we read textbooks to gather facts that would be included later on in a test (*study*). While facts are important in Bible reading, there's more. If you also want to get to know God or experience God, you'll need to explore the events a little more (*meditation*). Both study and meditation are valuable; here are the differences.

- Study (dissecting the text): What exactly is the text saying? What do the words mean?
- Meditation (savoring the text and entering into it): What is God saying to me? What is God inviting me to consider?

7

The advantage of meditating on scripture is that we not only get to know God better but also we are usually changed from the inside out. Our thoughts and feelings change, which then changes our behavior in an organic way. We want to grow as God is guiding us to be and to do differently. Meditating on scripture reorganizes our thoughts, feelings, and motives "so that you may be careful to act in accordance with all that is written in it. For then you shall make your way prosperous, and then you shall be successful" (Josh. 1:8).

Using the "Movie Method"

In this Advent study we will use what can be called "participative" meditation: you become a part of the story in some way. You participate in it through your imagination so that the event becomes a movie in your mind. This is, of course, how the Jews celebrate Passover—by entering the story as they eat the food and converse at the table. Christians have used participative meditation for centuries as well, especially those who have learned the Spiritual Exercises of Ignatius of Loyola, which guide people into experiences of Jesus' life through the prayerful use of the imagination.

In each session, you'll have a choice either to be a "fly on the wall" observing the events or to see yourself as a particular person in the story and experience it from that person's point of view. Let the Spirit guide you. Either way, close your eyes and try to sense what was happening. If you had been there, what would you have seen? Heard? Would you have tasted, touched, or smelled anything? How did these people probably feel? What might it have been like to be in their shoes?

During the "Responding to the Story" phases, you'll be asked to pray silently. If you can, try to *write* your prayer. It doesn't have to be long. Writing keeps your mind from wandering and helps you think more concretely, rather than letting thoughts get muddled in your mind. If writing prayers seems like *work* to you, try using colored pens or even drawing your prayer.

In "Take Two" options, you can choose a meditation from the week to enter again. You might choose the one that seemed to resonate with you the most. Or you might pick a passage you skipped or even one that did not resonate with you because you're more intrigued with it now.

Meditating on a passage a second time is usually a richer and deeper experience, even if you're sure the Spirit drained every last drop of inspiration from it the first time. The spirit of a "Take Two" is that of a hiker who has a favorite trail and loves to do it again. But you'll know the passage better this time, and probably receive more from it. Expect God to surprise you.

But I Don't Have an Imagination!

Most people have a vivid imagination but think they don't. To prove you have a vivid imagination, answer this question: Can you worry? If so, you have an imagination because you've asked yourself, *What if . . . ?* many times and come up with vivid answers.

Here's another example: Think of a lemon. Now think of cutting a lemon into four pieces. Now think about putting a piece of the lemon in your mouth—quick, what comes to mind? What's happening inside your mouth right now? Has your imagination kicked into gear based on the fuel from your past experiences of the sour taste and tartness of touching a lemon with your tongue? If so, you have a skilled imagination.

Perhaps you don't want to use your imagination because you're afraid it might get you into trouble. You've imagined yourself telling your boss what you *really* think! In that case, your imagination is still a gift from God, but it needs to be retrained to imagine God-stuff. The imagination's potential for misleading can be reconfigured by the mind of Christ, which Paul claims we possess (1 Cor. 2:16). Think of how Christ's mind was filled with stories, images, and hopes drawn from God's history with the people of God—you see that "imagination can become a penetrating force."[1] The more you do the meditations, the more skilled your imagination will become.

> *The more you do the meditations, the more skilled your imagination will become.*

The guideline for all spiritual disciplines is this: Do them as you can, not as you can't.

Your goal in meditation is simply to be with God in the experience, not to perfectly reconstruct the event or even to have an inspiring experience. So don't think you have to try hard to create a careful, detailed picture or feel deep feelings. The Cultural Cues will help you immerse yourself in the passage. They ground you in a concrete way—what am I seeing or smelling? Establish yourself in the setting and then move through the passage to let God speak to you.

Sometimes the whole scene may elude you, but a word from the passage or a word picture will stand out. If so, focus on that. The guideline for all spiritual disciplines is this: Do them as you can, not as you can't.

Centering Yourself During Quiet Moments

At the beginning of each group session, participants have time to quiet themselves. This practice allows us to let go of distractions, enter the story, and be attentive to the presence of God. Praying the same opening prayer each week creates a routine that calms racing minds.

Breathing deeply a few times will help you quiet yourself. This makes it easier to stay in the present moment and dismiss the "traffic in your head" (the events of the day, comments made to you, what you have to do later that night).

It also helps to relax body parts one by one: bending the neck, letting the arms go limp, relaxing the legs and ankles. Loosen each part from the inside out. This doesn't mean we are setting aside our minds, just redirecting them away from the busyness of daily life. This process prepares us to wait on the still, small voice of God.

If you really struggle to settle down, try this exercise, suggested by Richard J. Foster in *Celebration of Discipline*, or something similar:

Begin by placing your palms down as a symbolic indication of your desire to turn over any concerns you may have to God. Inwardly you may pray, "Lord, I give to you my anger toward

John. I release my fear of my dentist appointment this morning. I surrender my anxiety over not having enough money to pay the bills this month. I release my frustration over trying to find a baby-sitter for tonight." Whatever it is that weighs on your mind or is a concern to you, just say, "palms down." Release it. You may even feel a certain sense of release in your hands. After several moments of surrender, turn your palms up as a symbol of your desire to receive from the Lord. Perhaps you will pray silently: "Lord, I would like to receive your divine love for John, your peace about the dentist appointment, your patience, your joy."[2]

When you find yourself distracted, you may wish to jot down what distracts you—errands to run, people to call—so you can release those distractions for a few moments. The more you quiet yourself, the easier it becomes each time. It may take a little discipline at first, but once you begin adjusting to God's wavelength, expect to enjoy abiding there. The quiet will renew you, not bore you. When words are spoken, they have more value and weight because silence is so prized.

HOW TO USE THIS BOOK

Day 1 of each week introduces a passage from the biblical narrative. This is the day when small groups will meet; instructions for the group leader are embedded in each Day 1's content. Additional instructions are found in the Leader's Guide at the back of the book. Days 2 through 7 of each week focus either on a single event (perhaps viewed through the eyes of different characters) or on related events.

Small groups will experience Day 1 together, setting the stage for the upcoming week's meditations. If you are using the book on your own, simply adapt the process from each Day 1 for yourself or your family; it will give you a pattern for engaging with the biblical story over the next several days.

Preparing for Day 1 and the following days: Have your copy of this book for writing responses to questions and prayers. The leader for group sessions should provide Bibles, pens, pencils, and blank paper.

Guidelines for Daily Meditations

If you miss a day or two, don't worry. Do the meditations *as you can, not as you can't*. Here are some practical suggestions:

1. Find a quiet place and try to use that same space each time. Turn off your phone and put it out of reach. Sit or lie down in a way that works best for you. Most people like sitting in a chair with a straight back, placing feet flat on the floor and hands either gently clasped or placed on the knees. But you might find another position more comfortable, even lying down. Stay in the position you choose. This will decrease distractions and help you stay on track. Breathe deeply and relax. Notice the stillness and enjoy it. Remember that God is gazing at you with great love.

2. Read the opening prayer, either silently or aloud.

3. Follow the directions and ponder the passage presented to you. Picture the scene: see it, hear it, taste it, live in it. When your mind wanders, don't be discouraged. Gently come back to the passage.

4. Receive whatever comes to you. If nothing seems to come, this may have been a time for you to sit and simply enjoy God's presence.

5. Do try to write your prayer, even if it's only a word or two. If possible, discuss the experience with a friend.

Special Event

You or your group may wish to watch the movie *The Nativity Story*.[3] This movie can help you visualize life in rural Nazareth, the trip to Bethlehem, the daily lives and reactions of Mary, Joseph, Joseph's friends, Mary's parents, the shepherds, the wise men, and Herod. Let the film give your imagination a boost as you picture in your mind's eye the setting and characters of the Advent and Christmas stories.

EXPERIENCING THE BLESSING OF ZECHARIAH AND ELIZABETH

First Sunday of Advent
Zechariah's Surprise in the Temple *(Luke 1:5-25)*

Today you begin an Advent study that invites you to experience familiar biblical stories in a new way. The group leader will walk you through the preparation, scripture reading, and exercises below to help you engage with the scripture. For the rest of the week, follow the guidance for Days 2 through 7 about related Bible passages.

Opening Ourselves *(10 minutes)*

Once the group has gathered and is seated, the leader encourages everyone to relax and take a few deep breaths.

Pray this opening prayer:

> Let us release the cares of our day,
> and open our eyes to the wonder of God.
> With an attitude of empathy to people of another time,
> let us open our hearts and minds to God.
> Let us prepare to experience God's word to us
> through the presence of the Holy Spirit.[1]

Entering the Story *(20 minutes)*

Read today's scripture passage silently. In small-group settings, the leader will then read aloud the notes that follow the scripture. Review these notes yourself if you are not part of a group. Consider how this additional information affects your understanding of the story. Then close your eyes and listen as the leader reads the passage again (reread the passage aloud if you are on your own). Hear

---

LUKE 1:5-25

[5]In the days of King Herod of Judea, there was a priest named Zechariah, who belonged to the priestly order of Abijah. His wife was a descendant of Aaron, and her name was Elizabeth. [6]Both of them were righteous before God, living blamelessly according to all the commandments and regulations of the Lord. [7]But ***they had no children,*** because Elizabeth was barren, and both were getting on in years.

[8]Once when he was serving as priest before God and his section was on duty, [9]he was ***chosen by lot***, according to the custom of the priesthood, to enter the sanctuary of the Lord and ***offer incense***. [10]Now

Italicized Words & Phrases

they had no children In those times infertility was a source of great shame. It was considered a personal, domestic, and economic tragedy. This may have been more shameful for Zechariah and Elizabeth because Zechariah was a priest. Because children were and are considered to be a blessing from God, people assumed that an infertile couple was not blessed or did not deserve blessing. Zechariah was possibly sixty years old.[2]

chosen by lot Because every descendant of Aaron was a priest, there may have been about twenty thousand priests. As a result, priests did not get to serve very often and they looked forward to these times immensely.

offer incense Incense was offered before the daily morning sacrifice and after the evening sacrifice so that the "sacrifices might go up to God wrapped in an envelope of sweet-smelling incense."[3] Zechariah would have stood alone in the holy place with the altar of incense before him.[4] After lighting the incense, he would have bowed to worship, but he was interrupted.

at the time of the incense offering, the **whole assembly** of the people was praying outside. [11]Then there appeared to him an angel of the Lord, standing at the right side of the altar of incense. [12]When Zechariah saw him, he was terrified; and fear overwhelmed him. [13]But the angel said to him, "Do not be afraid, Zechariah, for your prayer has been heard. Your wife Elizabeth will bear you a son, and you will name him John. [14]You will have joy and gladness, and many will rejoice at his birth, [15]for he will be great in the sight of the Lord. He must never drink wine or strong drink; even before his birth he will be filled with the Holy Spirit. [16]He will turn many of the people of Israel to the Lord their God. [17]With the spirit and power of **Elijah** he will go before him, to **turn the hearts of parents to their children**, and the disobedient to the wisdom of the righteous, to make ready a people prepared for the Lord." [18]Zechariah said to the angel, "**How will I know that this is so?** For I am an old man, and my wife is getting on in years." [19]The angel replied, "I am **Gabriel.** I stand in the presence of God, and I have been sent to speak to you and to bring you this good news. [20]But now, because you did not believe my words, which will be fulfilled in their time, you will become mute, unable to speak, until the day these things occur."

[21]Meanwhile the people were waiting for Zechariah, and wondered at his delay in the sanctuary. [22]When he did come out, he could not speak to them, and they realized that he had seen a vision in the sanctuary. He kept motioning to them and remained unable to speak. [23]When his time of service was ended, he went to his home.

---

whole assembly Crowds waited outside in the Court of the Israelites for the priest to appear after the evening sacrifice and incense.

Elijah was considered the greatest of prophets, having been hidden during a drought and fed by ravens and then calling down fire from heaven on a sacrifice on Mount Carmel.

turn the hearts of parents to their children echoing the prophecy in Malachi 4:6

How will I know that this is so? Zechariah seems to be demanding a sign so he can be sure.

Gabriel also announced Jesus' birth to Mary a little later.

> [24]After those days his wife Elizabeth conceived, and for five months she remained in seclusion. She said, [25]"This is what the Lord has done for me when he looked favorably on me and took away the disgrace I have endured among my people."

the words as if they are new to you. Move deeper into the scene in your imagination on this second reading.

Write a sentence or two in response to these questions in the space below:

1. What feelings might Zechariah have had about being chosen by lot to enter the sanctuary of the Lord and offer incense? Perhaps thrilled? Or terrified?[5]

2. What thoughts or feelings or past experiences might have prompted Zechariah to ask, "How will I know that this is so?" (v. 18)?

3. What feelings might Zechariah have experienced when he kept motioning to the others and remained unable to speak (v. 22)? One commentator surmises that Zechariah was in a "wordless daze of joy."[6] What do you think? How would those emotions blend with the emotions he probably had in seeing a vision?

Here are some Cues to help you enter the story.

BIBLICAL CUE: *An Angel's Appearance*

In this passage we aren't told what Gabriel looked like, but elsewhere angels usually appeared clothed in white. Angels were so dazzling in appearance that they terrified those who saw them. Hence, they often began their message with the words "Do not be afraid" (Matt. 28:2-5).

HISTORICAL CUE: *The Altar of Incense*

Zechariah's eyes were probably already overwhelmed by the altar. If this altar was like the one in Solomon's Temple, it was built of wood and measured 18 by 18 by 36 inches. And it had horns! The altar's top and sides were overlaid with gold, and it was surrounded by a crown or rim of gold. For ease of transport it had golden rings.

SENSORY CUE: *Smell of Incense*

Incense mentioned in tabernacle and temple worship is generally "sweet incense," compounded in specific amounts with perfumes, pure frankincense, and various other ingredients[7] (Exod. 30:34-36). Frankincense emits a fragrance of pine and lemon combined with a dry, woody aroma.[8]

PICTURING CUE: *Talking with Your Hands*

How would you describe having seen an angel and being given a message if you could use only your hands and arms? Consider what it was like for an esteemed priest to do what might have looked to us moderns like a game of charades.

Responding to the Story *(15 minutes)*

As the leader reads the passage aloud, try to picture Zechariah, or even put yourself in his place, smelling the incense, seeing what he saw and feeling what he might have felt. If you wish, you can lie on the floor or prop your feet up on another chair.

- What do I (as Zechariah or observing Zechariah) hear or see?
- What feelings do I imagine Zechariah had?

- What word, phrase, scene, or image emerges from the scripture and stays with me?

Write your responses here.

Consider whether God is offering an invitation to you in this passage. Sit quietly for a few minutes, pondering these questions:

- How is my life touched today by this passage?
- Is there some idea, feeling, or intention I need to embrace from it? If so, what?
- What might God be inviting me to be or know or understand or feel or even do?

Be open to the quiet and don't feel pressured to come up with answers. Write thoughts prompted by the questions in the space below.

Take a few minutes to respond to God in prayer about any invitation or call from today's scripture. Reflect on this question:

- What do I most want to say to God about this experience in scripture?

Participants may wish to ask God questions (answers may come to them through the group or later in the week). They might want to write their prayer in the space below. That practice keeps the mind from wandering.

Allow time to sit in the quiet and consider:

- How did God (or God's actions) seem to me in this passage?
- What does this tell me about what God is like?

Spend a few minutes simply resting in God's presence.

Group Sharing *(10 minutes)*

Group participants may now share, if they wish, responses to this question:

- What do I think God might have been saying to me, calling me to be, to know or understand or feel or do?

If people choose not to share, that's fine. Listening to what others say may resonate with them. It's also interesting to see how God speaks to our sisters and brothers in Christ in a variety of ways.

Closing Prayer *(5 minutes)*

Close the session by praying the following prayer together as group members look forward to engaging scripture in the coming week. You all may want to use this prayer each day even if you don't do a meditation that day.

> Grant us wisdom and courage this week:
> to be open to your surprises, O God;
> to taste and see your presence in new ways;
> to trust that you will do good and joyful things in our lives
>   and in the world.

During the Week

Here are two practices or exercises to try in the coming week:

- Before going to bed, or when you're doing a simple chore (for example, taking out trash, washing dishes, locking doors before retiring), reflect on this: is there anything God might be leading me to *do* because of what came to me today in this passage?

  This must not be forced or contrived or according to the usual tapes that might play in your mind (for example, fix this person; make someone happy; correct people's thinking; strive a little harder). God may not be leading you to do anything; but if so, be open to what that might be.

- Observe older people you know and try to spot moments when they seem joyful or amused. Then ask in a playful way (if they aren't saying), "What are you smiling about today?" Or you can do this with anyone the Spirit leads you to.

  Consider the joys of older people. You might want to ask an older friend what makes him or her particularly happy. If you have an older friend who is particularly joyful, ask him or her what is required to be joyful as the years go by.

Day 2
Elizabeth Sees Zechariah's Strange Behavior
(Luke 1:5-25)

Settling In

Quiet yourself as in the group experience. Get in a relaxed position (as long as it won't allow you to fall asleep). Breathe in and out slowly a few times.

Place a bookmark at the beginning of Week One so you can refer to resources there. Pray the opening prayer on page 13.

Entering the Story

Read the passage (Luke 1:5-25) on pages 14–16 aloud slowly to yourself. (Or read it in another version of the Bible if you wish.)

Questions to Help You Enter the Story

Write a sentence or two in response to these questions:

1. What feelings might Elizabeth have had about Zechariah's being chosen by lot to enter the sanctuary of the Lord and offer incense? Consider that for decades Elizabeth has been forced to endure the disgrace of being childless (v. 25). For example, perhaps she thought, *Maybe we're not such losers after all*.

2. What might those five months of seclusion have been like
   for Elizabeth (v. 24)? With a husband who could not speak?

Review the Picturing Cues from the group meeting (p. 17) and consider this:

PICTURING CUE: *Watching People Talk with Their Hands*

Think of watching someone you know very well and whom you
love and have seen in all kinds of circumstances now talking with
his hands. You've never seen him do this before. What does his
facial expression look like? What are you thinking? What are
you feeling? Confused? Trying not to laugh? Exhausted trying to
understand him?

Responding to the Story

Read the passage aloud again, trying to picture yourself as Elizabeth, seeing what she saw and feeling what she might have felt. Or
you might be an observer, standing a few feet away.

- What do I (as Elizabeth or observing Elizabeth) hear or see?
- What word, phrase, scene, or image emerges from the scrip-
  ture and stays with me?
- What feelings do I imagine Elizabeth had?

Perhaps God is offering you an invitation in this passage to
enlarge your understanding in the next few days. In what way might
that be? Sit quietly for a few minutes, pondering these questions:

- How is my life touched today by this passage?
- Is there some idea, feeling, or intention I need to embrace
  from it? If so, what?
- What might God be inviting me to be or know or understand
  or feel or even do?

Take a few minutes to respond to God about this in prayer.

- What do I most want to say to God about this experience in
  scripture?

You may wish to ask God questions (the answers to which may come to you through the group or later in the week). You might want to write your prayer. Sometimes that keeps our minds from wandering.

Sit in the quiet and consider:

- How did God (or God's actions) seem to me in this passage? What does this tell me about what God is like?

Spend a few minutes simply resting in God's presence.
Finish by reciting the prayer of Ignatius of Loyola:

Take, Lord, and receive all my liberty, my memory, my under-
    standing and
my entire will—all I have and call my own.
You have given it all to me. To you, Lord, I return it.
Everything is yours; do with it what you will.
Give me only your love and your grace.
That is enough for me.[9]
Amen

Day 3
Faithful Pray-ers Wait Outside the Temple
(Luke 1:5-25)

Settling In

Quiet yourself as in the group experience. Get in a relaxed position (as long as it won't allow you to fall asleep). Breathe in and out
slowly a few times.

Place a bookmark at the beginning of Week One so you can
refer to resources there. Pray the opening prayer.

Entering the Story

Read the passage (Luke 1:5-25) on pages 14–16 aloud slowly to yourself. (Or read it in another version of the Bible if you wish.)

Questions to Help You Enter the Story

Write a sentence or two in response to these questions:

1. Imagine yourself as one of the people in this passage. You're at the Temple on an autumn morning. You're praying as the priest is offering incense. What kind of person might you be, to be doing this?

2. Can you imagine praying with all of these people in a group as a priest goes into the holiest place on earth? What might you have been praying in that circumstance such as, "I wonder what's happening. Zechariah is taking more time than usual."

3. If you had been one of these people, what might you have thought and felt when you realized that Zechariah had seen a vision?

PICTURING CUE: *Watching People Talk with Their Hands*

Think of what it might be like watching a priest you respect talking and motioning with his hands. You've never seen him do this before.

- What does his facial expression look like?
- What am I thinking?
- What am I feeling about Zechariah? about Elizabeth?

Responding to the Story

Read the passage aloud again, trying to picture yourself as one of these faithful pray-ers, sitting in the Temple, wondering what has happened to this priest. Maybe you want to leave and go home. Maybe you're afraid Zechariah has gotten sick. Or you might be an observer, standing a few feet away, watching them.

- What do I (as a praying Israelite or observing such people) hear or see?
- What word, phrase, scene, or image emerges from the scripture and stays with me?
- What feelings do I imagine some of these people had?

Perhaps God is offering you an invitation in this passage to enlarge your understanding in the next few days. In what way might that be? Sit quietly for a few minutes, pondering these questions:

- How is my life touched today by this passage?
- Is there some idea, feeling, or intention I need to embrace from it? If so, what?
- What might God be inviting me to be or know or understand or feel or even do?

Take a few minutes to respond to God about this in prayer.

- What do I most want to say to God about this experience in scripture?

You may wish to ask God questions (the answers to which may come to you through the group or later in the week). You might want to write your prayer in the space below.

Sit in the quiet and consider:

- How did God (or God's actions) seem to me in this passage? What does this tell me about what God is like?

Spend a few minutes simply resting in God's presence. Finish by reciting the prayer of Ignatius on page 22.

Day 4
The Angel's Point of View
(Luke 1:5-25)

Settling In

Quiet yourself. Get in a relaxed position. Breathe in and out slowly a few times.

Place a bookmark at the beginning of Week One so you can refer to resources there. Pray the opening prayer on page 13.

Entering the Story

Read the passage (Luke 1:5-25) on pages 14–16 aloud slowly to yourself. (Or read it in another version of the Bible if you wish.)

Questions to Help You Enter the Story

Write a sentence or two in response to these questions:

1. Gabriel's first words are a frequent command in scripture: "Don't be afraid." In fact, scholar N. T. Wright says it's the most frequent command in scripture.[9] What does this tell you about what Gabriel understood about Zechariah? About God's desires for Zechariah as Gabriel spoke with him?

2. Gabriel's announcement to Zechariah was 122 words long and full of good news (Luke 1:13-17). Pick out (underline) all the pieces of good news in his words. If Gabriel had human kinds of facial expressions, what expression might have accompanied these words?

3. Have you ever needed to bring good but startling and possibly disturbing news to people? If so, what was that like?

PICTURING CUE: *Appearance of an Angel*

In this passage we aren't told what Gabriel looked like, but elsewhere angels usually appeared clothed in white. They were so dazzling in appearance that they terrified those who saw them. This startling, heart-stopping vision is very different from the sweet, dreamy cherubs we often see portrayed in pictures.

Gabriel, in particular, is an announcing angel to Mary as well as to Zechariah. Gabriel was commissioned to explain to Daniel the vision of the ram and the he-goat, and to give the prediction of the seventy weeks (Dan. 8:16; 9:21). Think of various ways important announcements are made. How do elements of an angel's appearance signal to humans the gravity and majesty of their announcements?

Responding to the Story

Read the passage aloud again. You may not find it easy to imagine yourself in the place of Gabriel, but give it a try. Simply view the scene through Gabriel's eyes. Or you might want to be an unseen observer who watches Gabriel intently.

- What did Gabriel see and hear?
- What strikes me about Gabriel's appearance and way of being?
- What feelings do I imagine Gabriel had?
- What feelings do I imagine some of these people had?
- What word, phrase, scene, or image emerges from the scripture and stays with me?

Perhaps God is offering you an invitation in this passage to enlarge your understanding in the next few days. In what way might that be? Sit quietly for a few minutes, pondering these questions:

- How is my life touched today by this passage?
- Is there some idea, feeling, or intention I need to embrace from it? If so, what?
- What might God be inviting me to be or know or understand or feel or even do?

Take a few minutes to respond to God about this in prayer.

- What do I most want to say to God about this experience in scripture?

You may wish to ask God questions. You might want to write your prayer here.

Sit in the quiet and consider:

- How did God (or God's actions) seem to me in this passage? What does this tell me about what God is like?

Spend a few minutes simply resting in God's presence. Finish by reciting the prayer of Ignatius on page 22.

Day 5
John the Baptist Is Born
(Luke 1:57-66)

Settling In

Quiet yourself as in the group experience. Get in a relaxed position. Breathe in and out slowly a few times.

Pray the opening prayer on page 13.

Entering the Story

Read the passage (Luke 1:57-66) below silently. Then read the notes that follow. Think about how they affect the story. Then read the passage to yourself aloud, slowly, taking into consideration all the comments below.

LUKE 1:57-66

[57]Now the time came for Elizabeth to give birth, and she bore a son. [58]Her neighbors and relatives heard that the Lord had shown his great mercy to her, and they *rejoiced with her.*

[59]*On the eighth day they came to circumcise* the child, and they were going to name him Zechariah after his father. [60]But his mother said, "No; he is to be called John." [61]They said to her, "None of your relatives has this name."

[62]Then they began motioning to his father to find out what name he wanted to give him. [63]He asked for a writing tablet and wrote, "His name is John." And all of them were amazed.

[64]Immediately his mouth was opened and his tongue freed, and he began to speak, praising God. [65]Fear came over all their neighbors, and all these things were talked about throughout the entire hill country of Judea. [66]All who heard them pondered them and said, "What then will this child become?" For, indeed, the hand of the Lord was with him.

Italicized Words & Phrases

rejoiced with her When the time of a birth was near, friends and local musicians gathered. If the baby was a boy, the musicians began playing and the parents were congratulated.

On the eighth day they came to circumcise This special ceremony always occurred on the eighth day in the parents' home, and then the child was named.

CULTURAL CUE: *The Biggest Day of Her Life*

For women in this era, getting married was the point of life. Their greatest achievement was to give birth to a son. So while giving birth is special to many people, this birth would have made Elizabeth's life truly worth living.

PICTURING CUE: *Elizabeth Knew the Name*

At some point, Zechariah must have communicated to Elizabeth that the baby would be named John. (She may or may not have been able to read, so she would have had to ask someone to read what Zechariah wrote to her.) Try to picture how all this might have come about and how she readily trusted her husband (and knew her baby was a boy!).

Questions to Help You Enter the Story

Write a sentence or two in response to these questions:

1. What words (do I think) describe Elizabeth's physical condition on the day of her baby's birth? Consider her age.

2. What words (do I think) describe Elizabeth's emotional and mental condition on the day of her baby's circumcision ceremony in her home (eight days later)? Consider that her husband had not been able to communicate for nine months (including giving orders, which husbands did a lot of in those days). For months Elizabeth had taken care of all the negotiations and day-to-day matters that required a voice.

As you read the account, keep in mind this elated state of mind in a body that is giving birth. While Elizabeth was in this heightened physical and emotional state, people came to be with her and Zechariah to celebrate (houseguests?!), and she no doubt joined with them.

Responding to the Story

Read the passage aloud again. Imagine yourself in Elizabeth's place on these two days or try to observe Elizabeth. Consider her physical and emotional state.

- What do I (as Elizabeth or observing Elizabeth) hear or see?
- What word, phrase, scene, or image emerges from the scripture and stays with me?
- What feelings do I imagine Elizabeth had?

Perhaps God is offering you an invitation in this passage to enlarge your understanding in the next few days. In what way might that be? Sit quietly for a few minutes, pondering these questions:

- How is my life touched today by this passage?
- Is there some idea, feeling, or intention I need to embrace from it? If so, what?
- What might God be inviting me to be or know or understand or feel or even do?

Take a few minutes to respond to God about this in prayer. Try writing it.

- What do I most want to say to God about this experience in scripture?

Sit in the quiet and consider:

- How did God (or God's actions) seem to me in this passage? What does this tell me about what God is like?

Spend a few minutes simply resting in God's presence. Finish by reciting the prayer of Ignatius on page 22.

Day 6
Zechariah Imagines the Future
(Luke 1:67-79)

Settling In

Quiet yourself and breathe in and out slowly a few times.
   Pray the opening prayer on page 13.

Entering the Story

Read the passage (Luke 1:67-79) below silently. Then read the
notes that follow the scripture text. Think about how they affect
the story. Then read the passage to yourself aloud slowly, taking
into consideration all the comments.

LUKE 1:67-79

[67]Then his father Zechariah was filled with the Holy Spirit and spoke
this prophecy:
   [68] "Blessed be the Lord God of Israel, for he has looked favorably on
his people and *redeemed* them.
   [69] He has raised up a mighty savior for us in the house of his servant
David,
   [70] as he spoke through the mouth of his holy prophets from of old,
   [71] that we would be saved from our enemies and from the hand of
all who hate us.

Italicized Words & Phrases

redeemed to be rescued, to be bought back. Zechariah would have understood this to mean Israel's being freed from bondage to the Romans. John
also played a role in the redemption of our lives as we are freed from sin
and despair through the availability of life with God through confidence in
Christ.

72 Thus he has shown the mercy promised to our ancestors,
and has remembered his holy covenant,
73 the oath that he swore to our ancestor Abraham,
to grant us 74that we, being rescued from the hands of our ene-mies, might serve him without fear, 75in holiness and righteousness before him all our days.
76 And you, child, will be called the prophet of the Most High;
for you will go before the Lord to prepare his ways,
77 to give **knowledge** of **salvation** to his people by the forgiveness of their sins.
78 By the tender mercy of our God,
the dawn from on high will break upon us,
79 to give light to those who sit in darkness and in the shadow of death, to guide our feet into the way of peace."

---

knowledge The biblical idea of knowledge is interactive relationship.

salvation deliverance from danger in this life; healing and spiritual and eter-nal deliverance in the next life

BIBLICAL CUE: *Zechariah's Longing*

Zechariah wanted deliverance for Israel. Even though Israel had come back from the Babylonian captivity, they had never really been free from domination. "One evil empire after another had trampled [Israel] underfoot; now at last God was going to give them deliverance. We can feel the long years of pain and sorrow, of dark-ness and death, overshadowing his mind. Nameless enemies are lurking around the corner in [Zechariah's] imagination and expe-rience. No doubt it was partly this that had made him question Gabriel's word in the first place. . . . [Zechariah] has pondered the agony and the hope [of Israel] for many years, and . . . now finds the two bubbling out of him as he looks in awe and delight at his baby son."[10]

Questions to Help You Enter the Story

Write a sentence or two in response to these questions:

1. What words would you use to describe Zechariah's longing? What tone do you (think you) detect in this prophecy? What emotions might be behind it?

2. After nine months of silence, Zechariah is "filled with the Holy Spirit." What might that experience have been like for Zechariah?

3. Notice how Zechariah speaks directly to his son in verse 76. How does this compare to what people usually say to babies? What look might have been on Zechariah's face?

Optional Approach: Reread the passage. This time identify the ideas that draw you most by color-coding them with colored pens according to what you think works best. You might underline words in color or draw boxes or triangles around them.

Then look at what you did and answer these questions:

- Why did I choose those colors?
- What does each color seem to mean or represent?
- Might I need to understand or embrace these ideas at this moment in my life? If so, why?

Responding to the Story

Keeping the above exercise in mind, read the passage aloud, putting into it the emotions and desires Zechariah probably had.

- What word or phrase stands out to me or resonates with me?
- Why do I think that is?
- What might God be inviting me to understand or embrace, feel, or know?

Perhaps God is offering you an invitation in this passage to enlarge your understanding. In what way might that be? Sit quietly for a few minutes, pondering these questions:

- How is my life touched today by this passage?
- Is there some idea, feeling, or intention I need to embrace from it? If so, what?

Take a few minutes to respond to God about this in prayer.

- What do I most want to say to God about this experience in scripture?

You may wish to ask God questions. You may want to write your prayer in the space below.

Sit in the quiet and consider:

- How did God (or God's actions) come across to me in this passage? What does this tell me about what God is like?

Spend a few minutes simply resting in God's presence. Finish by reciting the prayer of Ignatius on page 22.

Day 7
Parents of a "Spirited" Boy
(Luke 1:80)

Settling In

Quiet yourself. Get in a relaxed position and breathe deeply a few times. Pray the opening prayer on page 13.

Entering the Story

Read the passage (Luke 1:80) below silently. Then read the notes below the scripture text. Think about how they affect the story. Then read the passage to yourself aloud, slowly, taking into consideration the comments.

LUKE 1:80

⁸⁰The child grew and became **strong in spirit**, and he was in the **wilderness** until the day he appeared publicly to Israel.

Italicized Words & Phrases

strong in spirit most likely, powerful in the Spirit of God, or perhaps simply "spirited"

wilderness probably the desert, and so a simple life close to nature. Perhaps, as Jesus had, John found the animals to be companions (Mark 1:13).

Questions to Help You Enter the Story

Write a sentence or two in response to these questions:

1. What would a child who is "strong in spirit" be like?

2. What might such a child be like to parent (especially for the elderly Zechariah and Elizabeth)?

3. What might it mean for me to become "strong in spirit" as John was?

Responding to the Story

Keeping the exercise above in mind, read the passage aloud, putting into it the emotions and desires Zechariah and Elizabeth probably had.

- What word or phrase stands out to me or resonates with me? Why do I think that is?

Perhaps God is offering you an invitation in this passage to enlarge your understanding. In what way might that be? Sit quietly for a few minutes, pondering these questions:

- How is my life touched today by this passage?
- Is there some idea, feeling, or intention I need to embrace from it? If so, what?
- What might God be inviting me to be or know or understand or feel or even do?

Take a few minutes to respond to God about this in prayer.

- What do I most want to say to God about this experience in scripture?

Say whatever you need to say to God.
Sit in the quiet and consider:

- How did God (or God's actions) came across to me in this passage? What does this tell me about what God is like?

Spend a few minutes resting in God's presence. Finish by reciting the prayer of Ignatius on page 22.

EXPERIENCING MARY'S PREPARATION

Second Sunday of Advent
Gabriel Visits Mary
(Luke 1:26-38)

Opening Ourselves *(10 minutes)*

Take a few deep breaths. Pray this prayer together:

> Let us release the cares of our day,
> and open our eyes to the wonder of God.
> With an attitude of empathy to people of another time,
> let us open our hearts and minds to God.
> Let us prepare to experience God's word to us
> through the presence of the Holy Spirit.

Entering the Story *(20 minutes)*

Read the session passage (Luke 1:26-38) below silently. The leader will then read the notes that follow the scripture text. Consider how they affect the story. Then close your eyes and listen as a group member reads the passage.

LUKE 1:26-38

[26]In the **sixth month** the angel Gabriel was sent by God to a town in Galilee called Nazareth, [27]to a virgin engaged to a man whose name was Joseph, of the house of David. **The virgin's name was Mary.**

[28]And he came to her and said, "Greetings, **favored one!** The Lord is with you." [29]But she was much perplexed by his words and pondered what sort of greeting this might be. [30]The angel said to her, "Do not be afraid, Mary, for you have found favor with God. [31]And now, you will conceive in your womb and bear a son, and you will name him **Jesus.** [32]He will be great, and will be called the Son of the Most High, and the Lord God will give to him the throne of his ancestor **David**. [33]He will reign over the house of Jacob forever, and of his kingdom there will be no end."

[34]Mary said to the angel, "How can this be, since I am a virgin?" [35]The angel said to her, "The Holy Spirit will come upon you, and the power of the Most High will overshadow you; therefore the child to be born will be holy; he will be called Son of God. [36]And now, your relative Elizabeth in her old age has also conceived a son; and this is the sixth month for her who was said to be barren. [37]For nothing will be impossible with God." [38]Then Mary said, "Here am I, the servant of the Lord; let it be with me according to your word." Then the angel departed from her.

Italicized Words & Phrases

sixth month of Elizabeth's pregnancy

The virgin's name was Mary. She was probably about fourteen or fifteen, and she had never had sex.

favored one! Mary's outward situation did not make her favored. Her family was poor and she lived in a small village in Galilee, which was not considered as pious and truly Jewish as Judea because its location on trade routes necessitated many associations with Gentiles.

Jesus means "Jehovah is salvation."[1]

David David fought the giant Goliath and later became a successful, God-loving king.

Questions to Help You Enter the Story

Write a sentence or two in response to these questions:

1. Mary was "much perplexed" by Gabriel's greeting (v. 29).
   The Message paraphrases Gabriel's words and ideas this way:

   Good morning!
   You're beautiful with God's beauty,
   Beautiful inside and out!
   God be with you.

   The Message concludes by saying that Mary "was thoroughly shaken, wondering what was behind a greeting like that" (v. 29). What expression would you guess appeared on her face? If you're willing, wear that expression on your face for your group (or look in a mirror). What feelings accompany this expression?

2. What color do you think of when you hear this phrase: "For nothing will be impossible with God" (v. 37)? Why?

3. Mary responds: "Here am I, the servant of the Lord; let it be with me according your word." If you were to put these words to music, what would the tune be like? Quick and cheerful? Slow and meditative? If there's a popular tune or hymn or even a singer you think it would fit well, what or who would that be?

Here are some related Cues on Day 5 of this Week (pp. 53–54):

BIBLICAL CUE: *"Magnificat" and the Great Inversion*
BIBLICAL AND HISTORICAL CUE: *What Mary Knew*
BIBLICAL AND HISTORICAL CUE: *What Mary Didn't Know (Future)*

Responding to the Story *(15 minutes)*

As the leader reads the passage aloud, try to picture Mary, or even put yourself in her place, seeing what she saw and feeling what she might have felt.

- What do I (as Mary or observing Mary) hear or see?
- What feelings do I have that Mary might have had?
- What word, phrase, scene, or image emerges from the scripture and stays with me?

Perhaps God is offering you an invitation in this passage to enlarge your understanding in the next few days. In what way might that be? Sit quietly for a few minutes, pondering these questions:

- How is my life touched today by this passage?
- Is there some idea, feeling, or intention I need to embrace from it? If so, what?
- What might God be inviting me to be or know or understand or feel or even do?
- Be open to the quiet, but don't feel pressured to come up with an answer.

Take a few minutes to respond to God about this in prayer.

■ What do I most want to say to God about this experience in scripture?

You may wish to ask God questions or write your prayer in the space below.

Sit in the quiet and consider:

■ How did God (or God's actions) seem to me in this passage? What does this tell me about what God is like?

Spend a few minutes simply resting in God's presence.

Group Sharing (10 minutes)

If you wish, share response to this question:

■ What do you think God might have been saying to you, inviting you to be or know or understand or feel or even do?

If you don't wish to speak, listen attentively to other group members to see if what they have to say relates to you and also to see how God speaks to our sisters and brothers in Christ differently than the way God speaks to us.

Closing Prayer (5 minutes)

Because "nothing will be impossible with God" (Luke 1:37), let us pray:
Grant us wisdom and courage this week to:
trust that nothing is impossible with God;
taste and see your presence in new ways;
trust that you will do good and joyful things in our lives and in the world.

During the Week

Here are two exercises to try in the coming week.

Before going to bed or when you're doing a relatively simple chore (taking out trash, washing dishes, locking doors before retiring), reflect on this:

- Is there anything God might be leading me to *do* because of what came to me today in this passage? This must not be forced or contrived or according to the usual tapes that might play in your mind (such as, fix this person; make someone happy; correct people's thinking; strive a little harder). God may not be leading you to do anything; but if so, be open to what that might be.
- Choose a song that expresses your deeper self. Intentionally bring this song into your day often. It may be Christmas-related or not, but think of a song that would help you absorb deep truths. Pick a task during which you can sing this song (drying your hair, shaving, letting your dog or cat out).

Notice how singing in the midst of ordinary life affects you.

Day 2
The Angel Speaks
(Luke 1:13-17, 19-20, 28, 30-33, 35-37)

Settling In

Quiet yourself as in the group experience. Get in a relaxed position. Breathe in and out slowly a few times.

Pray the opening prayer on page 13.

Entering the Story

Read the passages below silently. Then read the passages to yourself aloud slowly.

TO ZECHARIAH	TO MARY
Luke 1:13-17, 19-20	**Luke 1:28, 30-33, 35-37**

"**Do not be afraid**, Zechariah, for your prayer has been heard. Your wife Elizabeth will **bear you a son**, and **you will name him** John. [14]You will have joy and gladness, and many will rejoice at his birth, [15]for **he will be great** in the sight of the Lord. He must never drink wine or strong drink; even before his birth he will be filled with the **Holy Spirit**. [16]He will turn many of the people of Israel to the Lord their God. [17]With the spirit and power of Elijah he will go before him, to turn the hearts of parents to their children, and the disobedient to the wisdom of the righteous, to make ready a people prepared for the Lord." . . .

[19] "I am Gabriel. I stand in the presence of God, and I have been sent to speak to you and to bring you this good news. [20]But now, because you did not believe my words, which will be fulfilled in their time, you will become mute, unable to speak, until the day these things occur."

"Greetings, favored one! The Lord is with you." . . .

"**Do not be afraid**, Mary, for you have found favor with God. [31]And now, you will conceive in your womb and **bear a son**, and **you will name him** Jesus. [32]**He will be great**, and will be called the Son of the Most High, and the Lord God will give to him the throne of his ancestor David. [33]He will reign over the house of Jacob forever, and of his kingdom there will be no end." . . .

[35]"The **Holy Spirit** will come upon you, and the power of the Most High will overshadow you; therefore the child to be born will be holy; he will be called Son of God. [36]And now, your relative Elizabeth in her old age has also conceived a son; and this is the sixth month for her who was said to be barren. [37]For nothing will be impossible with God."

BIBLICAL COMPARISON CUE: *Comparing Gabriel's Words to Zecha-*
riah and to Mary

The phrases they have in common are italicized: *Do not be afraid;*
bear . . . a son; you will name him; he will be great; Holy Spirit.

Gabriel tells both Zechariah and Mary what their experiences
will be. Gabriel tells Zechariah that he will have joy and gladness,
and a bit about what John will be like. Gabriel tells Mary what
her experience will be in becoming pregnant and about Elizabeth's
situation. It seems Gabriel communicated what each needed to
know, but that was not always the same information.

CHARACTER CUE: *Mary's and Zechariah's Responses*

People often compare Mary's and Zechariah's responses to the
angel.

Mary: "Here am I, the servant of the Lord; let it be with me
according to your word."

Zechariah: "How will I know that this is so? For I am an old
man, and my wife is getting on in years."

Consider why Mary may have believed the angel more readily than Zechariah. How might their different ages and life experiences have affected them?

Questions to Help You Enter the Story

Write a sentence or two in response to these questions:

1. What was Gabriel's presence like? How might you have
   responded to such presence?

2. Notice that before Gabriel's remarkable statement that
   "nothing will be impossible with God," Gabriel offers an
   example of that truth: an older, infertile woman is pregnant.
   If Gabriel were to appear to you and say, "Nothing will be
   impossible with God," what might Gabriel use as an example

of that statement from your life or the lives of your acquaintances? Here are some possible examples:

- A certain person you love is now drug-free.
- You recovered from a heartbreaking situation or medical problem.
- You achieved or completed something you did not think was possible.
- Name your own.

BIBLICAL CONTEXT CUE: *Gabriel's Attitude*

If you were Gabriel planning to visit Zechariah and Mary, what attitude or manner would be appropriate or might work best? Remember that you are announcing events that will be the greatest shock of these people's lives.

Consider also that Gabriel knows he's representing God not only in message but in attitude. God is love, and even when difficult truths must be spoken, God no doubt would not stray from the principle of speaking the truth in love (Eph. 4:15). Perhaps Gabriel was excited. The right time had come (Gal. 4:4) for God's mystery of Christ to unfold (Eph. 1:9-10; Col. 2:2; 4:3).

Responding to the Story

Read the two passages aloud again. Imagine yourself in Gabriel's place or as a fly on the wall observing Gabriel.

- What do I (as Gabriel or observing Gabriel) hear or see?
- If angels have feelings, what might they have been?
- What word, phrase, scene, or image emerges from the scripture and stays with me?

Perhaps God is offering you an invitation in this passage to enlarge your understanding in the next few days. In what way might that be? Sit quietly for a few minutes, pondering these questions:

- How is my life touched today by this passage?
- Is there some idea, feeling, or intention I need to embrace from it? If so, what?
- What might God be inviting me to be or know or understand or feel or even do?

Take a few minutes to respond to God about this in prayer.

- What do I most want to say to God about this experience in scripture?

You may wish to ask God questions or write your prayer in the space below.

Sit in the quiet and consider:

- How did God (or God's actions) seem to me in this passage? What does this tell me about what God is like?

Spend a few minutes simply resting in God's presence. Finish by reciting the prayer of Ignatius on page 22.

Day 3
Mary Visits Elizabeth
(Luke 1:39-45, 56)

Settling In

Quiet yourself. Get in a relaxed position and breathe slowly.
    Pray the opening prayer on page 13.

Entering the Story

Read the passage below (Luke 1:39-45, 56) silently. Then read the notes that follow the scripture text. Think about how they affect the story from Mary's point of view. Then read the passage to yourself aloud slowly, taking into consideration all the comments below.

LUKE 1:39-45, 56

³⁹In those days Mary set out and **went with haste to a Judean town in the hill country**, ⁴⁰where she entered the house of Zechariah and greeted Elizabeth. ⁴¹When Elizabeth heard Mary's greeting, the child leaped in her womb. And Elizabeth was filled with the Holy Spirit ⁴²and exclaimed with a loud cry, "**Blessed** are you among women, and blessed is the fruit of your womb. ⁴³And why has this happened to me, that the mother of my Lord comes to me? ⁴⁴For as soon as I heard the sound of your greeting, the child in my womb leaped for joy. ⁴⁵And **blessed** is she who believed that there would be a fulfillment of what was spoken to her by the Lord." . . .

⁵⁶And Mary remained with her about three months and then returned to her home.

Italicized Words & Phrases

went with haste to a Judean town in the hill country This journey from northern Galilee to Judea would have taken about four to five days.[2]

Blessed (*makarios*) refers to the highest yet deepest type of current and eternal well-being possible for human beings, but it is also the term the Greeks used for the kind of blissful existence characteristic of the gods.[3]

blessed Elizabeth seems to be referring to herself here.

CULTURAL CUE: *Picturing the Differences*

While Elizabeth was probably about sixty years old, Mary would have been about fourteen. While Elizabeth was the wife of a priest and lived in the hill country of Judea, not far from Jerusalem—the Holy City, Mount Zion—Mary was a poor Galilean peasant who lived by those trade routes, tainted by associations with Gentiles.

Elizabeth was quick to believe the unbelievable news about Mary. Did Gabriel appear to her as well, or did she know Mary was "the mother of my Lord" because she was "filled with the Holy Spirit"? We don't know, but what do you think?

PICTURING CUE: *Two Pregnant Women*

Think about what it was like for these two women to manage. Elizabeth was an elderly woman who was six to nine months pregnant. She may have been very fragile. Was Zechariah trying to do everything?

Mary would have been in that first trimester when miscarriages often occur. However, Mary was poor so she wasn't used to being pampered. Did she get up to do things for Elizabeth only to have Elizabeth tell her to sit down, that she too needed to rest? Did Zechariah hire someone to help them?

Questions to Help You Enter the Story

Write a sentence or two in response to these questions:

1. How do I think Mary benefited from her time with Elizabeth?

2. What might they have talked about?

3. How might Mary have been tempted not to feel so "blessed"?

Responding to the Story

Read the passage aloud again. Imagine yourself in Mary's place, or observing this young woman. Consider her physical and emotional state after traveling so far from home.

- What do I (as Mary or observing Mary) hear or see?
- What word, phrase, scene, or image emerges from the scripture and stays with me?
- What feelings do I imagine Mary had that resonate with me?

Perhaps God is offering you an invitation in this passage to enlarge your understanding in the next few days. In what way might that be? Sit quietly for a few minutes, pondering these questions:

- How is my life touched today by this passage?
- Is there some idea, feeling, or intention I need to embrace from it? If so, what?
- What might God be inviting me to be or know or understand or feel or even do?

Take a few minutes to respond to God about this in prayer.

- What do I most want to say to God about this experience in scripture?

Say whatever you need to say to God.
Sit in the quiet and consider:

- How did God (or God's actions) seem to me in this passage? What does this tell me about what God is like?

Spend a few minutes simply resting in God's presence. Finish by reciting the prayer of Ignatius on page 22.

Day 4
Elizabeth Responds to Mary's Visit
(Luke 1:39-45, 56)

Settling In

Quiet yourself. Get in a relaxed position and breathe slowly.
Pray the opening prayer on page 13.

Entering the Story

Read the passage from Day 3 on p. 47 (Luke 1:39-45, 56) silently. (You may wish to read it from another Bible version this time.)

Then read the notes that follow the scripture text. Think about
how they affect the story from Elizabeth's point of view. Then read
the passage to yourself aloud slowly, taking into consideration all
the comments below and the Cultural Cues about their differences.

PICTURING CUE: *Elizabeth and Mary's Relationship*

Mary probably knew Elizabeth from the times her family traveled to
Jerusalem for feast days (usually three times a year). But now they
spoke as woman to woman about a divine mystery neither of them
clearly understood, and probably knew they didn't understand.
They probably were like any two women sharing secrets. Notice
how the word *blessed* is used twice and Elizabeth said the baby
jumped for *joy*. These two must have had happy times together.
What a gift to Elizabeth, who had had a sad life of rejection, and to
Mary, whose future life would be full of rejection and hard times.

PICTURING CUE: *Elizabeth's Adventure*

Think about the things that happened to Elizabeth or that she
seemed to *just do*, with little intentionality on her part:

- Her baby jumped inside her.
- She spoke divine truth that seemed to come from nowhere.
- She was filled with the Holy Spirit.

See also Day 3 cues on pages 47–48.

CULTURAL CLUE: *Picturing the Differences*

PICTURING CUE: *Two Pregnant Women*

Questions to Help You Enter the Story

Write a sentence or two in response to these questions:

1. What feelings might Elizabeth have experienced in light
   of her "adventure" (Picturing Cue: *Elizabeth's Adventure*
   [above])? Consider specifically her feelings about the situation, about herself (after previously feeling so unblessed),
   and about her future.

2. When have you had "happy times" with someone you did not know well (for example, a cousin at a family reunion, a church member on a long bus ride, someone who visited you when you were sick)?

Responding to the Story

Read the passage aloud again. Imagine yourself in Elizabeth's place or as someone observing her. Consider her physical and emotional state (six months pregnant, rejoicing that she is pregnant, having to navigate her world with a husband who can't talk).

- What do I (as Elizabeth or observing Elizabeth) hear or see?
- What word, phrase, scene, or image emerges from the scripture and stays with me?
- What feelings do I imagine Elizabeth had that resonate with me?

Perhaps God is offering you an invitation in this passage to enlarge your understanding in the next few days. In what way might that be? Sit quietly for a few minutes, pondering these questions:

- How is my life touched today by this passage?
- Is there some idea, feeling, or intention I need to embrace from it? If so, what?
- What might God be inviting me to be or know or understand or feel or even do?

Take a few minutes to respond to God about this in prayer.

- What do I most want to say to God about this experience in scripture?

Say whatever you need to say to God.
Sit in the quiet and consider:

- How did God (or God's actions) seem to me in this passage? What does this tell me about what God is like?

Spend a few minutes simply resting in God's presence. Finish by reciting the prayer of Ignatius on page 22.

Day 5
Mary Sings the Magnificat
(Luke 1:46-55)

Settling In

Quiet yourself. Breathe in and out slowly a few times.

Pray the opening prayer on page 13.

Entering The Story

Read the passage (Luke 1:46-55) below silently. Then read the notes that follow the scripture text. Think about how they affect the story. Then read the passage to yourself aloud slowly, taking into consideration all the comments below.

LUKE 1:46-55

[46]And Mary said,
"My soul ***magnifies*** the Lord,
[47] and my spirit ***rejoices*** in God my Savior,
[48] for he has looked with favor on the ***lowliness*** of his servant.
Surely, from now on all generations will call me blessed;
[49] for ***the Mighty One*** has done great things for me,
　　and holy is his name.

Italicized Words & Phrases

---

magnifies makes great[4]; praises

rejoices "I'm dancing the song of my Savior God" (v. 47, *The Message*).

lowliness a poor girl from the less prestigious part of an oppressed nation

the Mighty One powerful

⁵⁰ His mercy is for those who **fear** him
     from generation to generation.
⁵¹ He has shown strength with **his arm**;
     he has scattered the proud in the thoughts of their hearts.
⁵² He has brought down the powerful from their thrones,
     and lifted up the lowly;
⁵³ he has **filled the hungry** with good things,
     and sent the rich away empty.
⁵⁴ He has helped his servant Israel,
     in remembrance of his mercy,
⁵⁵ according to the **promise** he made to our ancestors,
     to Abraham and to his descendants forever."

---

fear "to cherish reverence and respect for" God; to honor God "lovingly by avoiding what is contrary to [God's] will and by striving after what pleases [God]"[5]

[God's] arm a symbol for power (Isa. 63:12)

filled the hungry satisfied those in dire need

promise salvation is available to all the nations of the earth (Gen. 17:19; 22:18).

BIBLICAL CUE: *"Magnificat" and the Great Inversion*

This song is traditionally called "the *Magnificat*," which is Latin for "magnifies." The Great Inversion "lies at the heart of the good news (or gospel) of Jesus and his people. . . . a general structure that permeates the message of the Bible as a whole and the reality portrayed therein. . . . There are none in the humanly 'down' position so low that they cannot be lifted up by entering God's order, and none in the humanly 'up' position so high that they can disregard God's point of view on their lives."[6] In other words, the first shall be last and the last shall be first (Mark 10:31).

BIBLICAL AND HISTORICAL CUE: *What Mary Knew*

Mary did not know exactly what Jesus would be, but she knew that he would fulfill promises made to Abraham, that through her son, "all the families of the earth shall be blessed" (Gen. 12:3). Gabriel's words echoed in her mind ("He will be great, and will be called the Son of the Most High, and the Lord God will give to him the throne of his ancestor David. He will reign over the house of Jacob forever, and of his kingdom there will be no end" [Luke 1:32-33]). Her son would ascend to King David's throne in place of their current "king," Herod, who was not a godly person. Somehow her son held the key to it all!

BIBLICAL AND HISTORICAL CUE: *What Mary Didn't Know (Future)*

What Mary didn't know (even though she sang of it) was that in her son's name, his followers would specialize in feeding the hungry (Luke 1:53). The "bride" of Christ (the church) would outlast all the great empires and reach the ends of the earth.

Questions to Help You Enter the Story

Write a sentence or two in response to these questions:

1. What kind of attitude did Mary seem to have in this song?

2. What sort of tune might go with this song? (What song do you already know that typifies the spirit of this song?)

3. If a person were to dance to this song, what would the dance be like? (Feel free to try out a few steps.)

Responding to the Story

Read the passage aloud again. Imagine yourself in Mary's place or observing her. Consider her physical and emotional state.

- What do I (as Mary or observing Mary) hear or see?
- What word, phrase, scene, or image emerges from the scripture and stays with me?
- What feelings do I imagine Mary had that resonate with me?

Perhaps God is offering you an invitation in this passage to enlarge your understanding. In what way might that be? Sit quietly for a few minutes, pondering these questions as needed:

- How is my life touched today by this passage?
- Is there some idea, feeling, or intention I need to embrace from it? If so, what?
- What might God be inviting me to be or know or understand or feel or even do?

Take a few minutes to respond to God about this in prayer.

- What do I most want to say to God about this experience in scripture?

Say whatever you need to say to God.
Sit in the quiet and consider:

- How did God (or God's actions) seem to me in this passage? What does this tell me about what God is like?

Spend a few minutes simply resting in God's presence. Finish by reciting the prayer of Ignatius on page 22.

Day 6
Mary Sings Hannah's Song
(1 Samuel 2:1-10; Luke 1:46-55)

Settling In

Quiet yourself. Get in a relaxed position and breathe deeply a few times.

Pray the opening prayer on page 13.

Entering the Story

Before reading the scripture, read these Cues:

BIBLICAL AND CULTURAL CUES: *Who Was Hannah and Why Did Mary Emulate Her?*

Hannah: A brave, industrious woman who became the mother of Samuel the prophet. She was childless for years and heartbroken. She prayed and asked God for a child. After she gave birth to Samuel, she sang the song on the left below. Part of the victory she sang about was that she was no longer looked down upon for being childless (especially by her husband's other wife, Peninnah). "Her rival used to provoke her severely, to irritate her, because the LORD had closed her womb" (1 Sam. 1:6). So she was victorious over those who degraded her.

Mary: Young Jewish girls often sang songs as they did their household tasks. It's thought that Hannah's song was one they sang. Here Mary (who probably knew the song well) adapted it in a moment of joy in praising God. Part of her "victory" was that she understood that her child would help deliver the people she loved, Israel.

Before reading Hannah's song on the left, picture a woman with a child she loves. She feels victorious. Please read the song aloud and, if possible, say it with the gusto with which Hannah probably sang it.

Read Hannah's song below on the left silently. Then read Mary's song on the right.

HANNAH'S SONG	MARY'S SONG
(1 Samuel 2:1-10)	(Luke 1:46-55)

HANNAH'S SONG

(1 Samuel 2:1-10)

¹Hannah prayed and said,
"My heart exults in the LORD;
my strength is exalted in my God.
My mouth derides my enemies,
because I rejoice in my victory.
² There is no Holy One like the LORD,
no one besides you;
there is no Rock like our God.
³ **Talk no more so very proudly**,
let not arrogance come from your mouth;
for the LORD is a God of knowledge,
and by him actions are weighed.
⁴ The bows of the mighty are broken,
but the feeble gird on strength.
⁵ Those who were full have hired themselves out for bread,
but **those who were hungry are fat with spoil**.
The barren has borne seven,
but she who has many children is forlorn.

MARY'S SONG

(Luke 1:46-55)

⁴⁶And Mary said,
"My soul magnifies the Lord,
⁴⁷ and my spirit rejoices in God my Savior,
⁴⁸ for he has looked with favor on the lowliness of his servant.
Surely, from now on all generations will call me blessed;
⁴⁹ for the Mighty One has done great things for me, and holy is his name.
⁵⁰ His mercy is for those who fear him
from generation to generation.
⁵¹ He has shown strength with his arm;
he has scattered the proud in the thoughts of their hearts.
⁵² He has brought down the powerful from their thrones, and **lifted up the lowly;**

⁶ The Lord kills and brings to life;
he brings down to Sheol and raises
   up.
⁷ The Lord makes poor and makes
   rich;
he brings low, he also exalts.
⁸ He raises up the poor from the
   dust;
he **lifts the needy from the ash
   heap**,
to make them sit with princes
and inherit a seat of honor.
For the pillars of the earth are the
   Lord's,
and on them he has set the world.
⁹ He will guard the feet of his faithful ones,
but the wicked shall be cut off in
   darkness;
for not by might does one prevail.
¹⁰ The Lord! His adversaries shall
   be shattered;
the Most High will thunder in
   heaven.
The Lord will judge the ends of the
   earth;
he will give strength to his king,
and exalt the power of his
   anointed."

**⁵³ he has filled the hungry with
   good things,**
and sent the rich away empty.
⁵⁴ He has helped his servant Israel,
in remembrance of his mercy,
⁵⁵ according to the promise he
   made to our ancestors,
to Abraham and to his descen-
   dants forever."

Italicized Words & Phrases

The italicized words and phrases indicate common ideas and similar wording in these two songs.

Hannah	Mary
My heart exults in the LORD; . . . because I rejoice in my victory. God as "Holy One"	My soul magnifies the Lord, and my spirit rejoices in God my Savior, God as Mighty One
Talk no more so very proudly, let not arrogance come from your mouth (v. 3)	he has scattered the proud in the thoughts of their hearts (v. 51)
those who were hungry are fat with spoil (v. 5)	he has filled the hungry with good things, (v. 53)
he lifts the needy from the ash heap (v. 8)	lifted up the lowly (v. 52)

If you spot others, underline them above.

Questions to Help You Enter the Story

Write a sentence or two in response to these questions:

1. If you are like most people (including the young Jewish girls of Mary's day), songs come into your mind when you're working, driving, puttering in the garage, or cleaning up your kitchen. What songs are they (maybe pop songs, childhood songs, other)?

2. Is there a song that expresses your deeper self that you could intentionally insert into your day more often? This might be a song that would help you absorb deep truths you really need to take in, or a Christmas song that moves you that you could intentionally sing or hum as Mary probably did.

3. Which themes from the songs are most meaningful for you today?

- Freedom from domination (victory)
- Celebrating God's greatness
- Celebrating God's strength (and empowerment of people like you)
- Joy that destructiveness in some form (for example, sickness, oppression, mental impairment) is not prevailing
- Celebrating that people who have suffered no longer suffer
- Other:

PICTURING CUE: *Elizabeth Watching Mary*

Elizabeth no doubt knew Hannah's song too. Picture her smiling as she listens to Mary's new version of an old, old song.

Responding to the Story

Read the passage aloud again. Imagine yourself in Mary's place hauling water or some other daily task or observing her doing this and singing. Consider her physical and emotional state.

- What do I (as Mary or observing Mary) hear or see?
- What word, phrase, or image emerges from the scripture and stays with me?
- What feelings do I imagine she had that resonate with me?

Perhaps God is offering you an invitation in this passage to enlarge your understanding. In what way might that be? Sit quietly for a few minutes, pondering these questions as needed:

- How is my life touched today by this passage?
- Is there some idea, feeling, or intention I need to embrace from it? If so, what?

- What might God be inviting me to be or know or understand or feel or even do?

Take a few minutes to respond to God about this in prayer.

- What do I most want to say to God about this experience in scripture?

Say whatever you need to say to God.

Sit in the quiet and consider:

- How did God (or God's actions) seem to me in this passage? What does this tell me about what God is like?

Spend a few minutes simply resting in God's presence. Finish by reciting the prayer of Ignatius on page 22.

Day 7
Take Two

Settling In

Quiet yourself and breathe in and out slowly a few times.
Pray the opening prayer on page 13.

Entering the Story

Think back over this week's meditations. Which one would you like to experience again? Maybe it was the one you seemed to resonate with the most. Or perhaps it was the one you liked or understood the least, and you'd like to try it again now that you've done a few more meditations.

Meditations to choose from in Week 2, Experiencing Mary's Preparation:

- Day 1: Gabriel Visits Mary (Luke 1:26-38), page 37.
- Day 2: The Angel Speaks (Luke 1:28, 30-33, 35-37 compared to Luke 1:13-17, 19-20), page 42.
- Day 3: Mary Visits Elizabeth (Luke 1:39-45, 56), page 46.
- Day 4: Elizabeth Responds to Mary's Visit (Luke 1:39-45, 56), page 49.
- Day 5: Mary Sings the Magnificat (Luke 1:46-55), page 52.
- Day 6: Mary Sings Hannah's Song (Luke 1:46-55 compared to 1 Samuel 2:1-10), page 56.

EXPERIENCING JOSEPH'S CHALLENGE

Third Sunday of Advent
Joseph "the Just" and His Dreams
(Matthew 1:18-25)

Opening Ourselves *(10 minutes)*

Take a few deep breaths. Pray this opening prayer together:

> Let us release the cares of our day,
> and open our eyes to the wonder of God.
> With an attitude of empathy to people of another time,
> let us open our hearts and minds to God.
> Let us prepare to experience God's word to us
> through the presence of the Holy Spirit.

Entering the Story *(20 minutes)*

Read the passage below silently. Then read the notes that follow the scripture text. Think about how they affect the story. Then read the passage to yourself aloud slowly, taking into consideration all the comments below.

Matthew 1:18-25

[18]Now the birth of Jesus the Messiah took place in this way. When his mother Mary had been engaged to Joseph, but before they lived together, she was found to be **with child from the Holy Spirit**. [19]Her husband Joseph, being a **righteous** man and **unwilling to expose her to public disgrace, planned to dismiss her quietly.** [20]But just when he had **resolved** to do this, an angel of the Lord appeared to him in a dream and said, "Joseph, son of David, do not be afraid to take Mary as your wife, for the child conceived in her is from the Holy Spirit. [21]She will bear a son, and you are to name him Jesus, for he will save his people from their sins." [22]All this took place to fulfill what had been spoken by the Lord through the **prophet**:

[23] "Look, the virgin shall conceive and bear a son, and they shall name him Emmanuel," which means, "God is with us."

[24]When Joseph awoke from sleep, he did as the angel of the Lord commanded him; he took her as his wife, [25]but had no marital relations with her until she had borne a son; and he named him Jesus.

Italicized Words & Phrases

with child from the Holy Spirit Mary was pregnant but still a virgin. (She hadn't had marital relations with a man.) She conceived this child from the Holy Spirit. If this sounds mysterious to you, it should. It's a mystery of the faith.

unwilling to expose her to public disgrace, planned to dismiss her quietly Joseph did not expose her as an adulteress but arranged for a quiet divorce.

the prophet Isaiah, as recorded in Isaiah 7:14

CULTURAL CUE: *Betrothal and Marriage Customs*

"From that moment [of engagement] Mary was the betrothed wife of Joseph; their relationship as sacred as if they had already been wedded. Any breach of it would be treated as adultery; nor could the bond be dissolved except, as after marriage, by regular divorce. Yet months might intervene between the betrothal and marriage."[1]

CHARACTER CUE: *Joseph "the Just"*

Because the word **righteous** in verse 19 (bold print) also has been translated "just" (KJV, NKJV, NLT), Joseph is sometimes referred to as "Joseph the Just." When we think of a "just" person, we think of someone who obeys laws and applies rules fairly to all. Joseph did not do as the law required: "If there is a young woman, a virgin already engaged to be married, and a man meets her in the town and lies with her, you shall bring both of them to the gate of that town and stone them to death" (Deut. 22:23-24). Joseph decided to break the law of Moses and divorce Mary quietly rather than publicly exposing her. Was that unjust? No, as this fact is related in Matthew 1:18-19, the text says Joseph was just. "Joseph clearly applied an extraordinary and unexpected definition of justice to this crisis with Mary. Justice for him was more than 'the equal application of law.'"[2]

CHARACTER CUE: *Joseph's Feelings*

Possibly Joseph fumed over this situation. Notice the word in bold in verse 20: **resolved**. Other versions say that Joseph "considered" or "thought about." Scholar Kenneth Bailey thinks these translations are legitimate but misleading. The Greek word (*enthymeomai*) has two meanings. It can mean to consider or think about; or it can mean becoming *very upset*. In other places in the New Testament, versions of *enthymeomai* are translated "wrath" and "rage." Very likely, Joseph was enraged. Bailey wonders if our admiration of Joseph has led us to discount the "very upset" translation. Do we really believe that when he found out his fiancée was pregnant, he sat quietly and "considered" this matter? Or would he naturally have felt deeply disappointed and indeed angry? Even though he showed mercy to Mary, he could still have been very upset or angry.[3] If he was angry, it's impressive that he seems to have reprocessed this anger into grace. He chose not be accusative but restorative. "He possessed the boldness, daring, courage and strength of character to stand up against his entire community and take Mary as his wife. He did so in spite of forces that no doubt wanted her stoned. His vision of justice stayed his hand."[4]

PICTURING CUE: *Joseph as a Carpenter*

Carpenters in those days were also stonemasons, versatile construction workers, and even artisans. Joseph and his own father (if alive) would no doubt have worked in ancient Sepphoris (four miles north of Nazareth), which was the chief city and capital of Galilee. In this city of thirty thousand, Herod was building a palace and theater.[5] Construction workers had a steady supply of work there.

Questions to Help You Enter the Story

Write a sentence or two in response to these questions:

1. If Joseph's fears of public disgrace led to anger, what might have been his angry thoughts?

- *How could Mary betray me?*
- *People will know about this; will I get work?*
- *I have lost the respect of my friends. She has shamed me!*
- *I thought I had good judgment about people. How could I have been so wrong?*
- Other:

2. Consider how fear often leads to anger:

Disagreeable Circumstance	Fear	Resulting Anger
Someone cuts you off while you're driving	fear of an accident	anger at driver
Your friend stops calling you or wanting to be with you	fear of losing friendship	anger at friend: Why won't he/she talk to me? Feeling betrayed
You come down with a disease	fear of sickness or even death	anger: How could this happen to me?

When, if ever, have you experienced or seen an angry person reprocess anger into grace? Perhaps you have seen someone choose to be restorative instead of accusative? When you think about this, what feeling comes over you?

Responding to the Story (15 minutes)

As the leader reads the passage aloud, try to picture Joseph and observe him, or even put yourself in his place, seeing what he saw and feeling what he might have felt.

- What do I (as Joseph or observing Joseph) hear or see?
- What feelings do I imagine Joseph had?
- What word, phrase, scene, or image emerges from the scripture and stays with me?

Perhaps God is offering you an invitation in this passage to enlarge your understanding in the next few days. In what way might that be?

Sit quietly for a few minutes, pondering these questions:

- How is my life touched today by this passage?
- Is there some idea, feeling, or intention I need to embrace from it? If so, what?
- What might God be inviting me to be or know or understand or feel or even do?

Be open to the quiet, but don't feel pressured to come up with an answer. Use this space to write anything you wish to:

Take a few minutes to respond to God in prayer.

- What do I most want to say to God about this experience in scripture?

You may wish to ask God questions (the answers to which may come to you through the group or later in the week). You might write your prayer in the space below.

Sit in the quiet and consider:

- How did God (or God's actions) seem to me in this passage? What does this tell me about what God is like?

Spend a few minutes simply resting in God's presence.

Group Sharing *(10 minutes)*

If you wish, share what you think God might have been saying to you, inviting you to be or know or understand or feel or even do. If you don't wish to speak, listen to the others. You may find that what they say relates to you. It's also interesting to see how God speaks to our sisters and brothers in Christ differently from the way God speaks to us.

Closing Prayer *(5 minutes)*

Grant us wisdom and courage this week:
    to trust you to guide us through difficult circumstances;
    to taste and see your presence in new ways;
    to trust that you will do good and joyful things in our lives and
    in the world.

During the Week

Before going to bed or when you're doing a relatively simple chore (taking out trash, washing dishes, locking doors before retiring), reflect on this: Is there anything God might be leading me to *do* because of what came to me today in this passage?

This must not be forced or contrived or according to the usual tapes that might play in your mind (such as, fix this person; make

someone happy; correct people's thinking; strive a little harder).
God may not be leading you to do anything; but if so, be open to
what that might be.

Project: Look for an opportunity to reprocess anger into grace.
Here are some ideas.
  When shopping this week,

- someone might be rude to you. You might look them directly
  in the eyes and grin.
- you might be annoyed with a salesclerk. You might instead
  say, "I know you're busy. Thank you for waiting on me."

Or do a kindness (small ones are fine) for someone you tend
to dismiss or even resent. For example, you might brush the snow
off someone's car in the church parking lot. Or ask, "How is your
[son, daughter, grandchild, dog, cat, rosebush, model train] doing
these days?"
  This won't be "faking it" if you plan this action now and ask
God to help you. In that moment, the Spirit will come alongside
you and empower you.

Day 2
Mary Experiences Joseph's Decisions
(Matthew 1:18-25)

Settling In

Quiet yourself as in the group experience. Get in a relaxed position (as long as it won't allow you to fall asleep). Breathe in and out
slowly a few times.
  Pray the opening prayer on page 13.

Entering the Story

Read the passage (Matt. 1:18-25) on page 64 above silently. Then
read the notes that follow the scripture text and the Cues above as

well as these Historical and Cultural Cues. Consider this time how Mary might have experienced Joseph's dream and decision not to divorce her.

HISTORICAL CUE: *Joseph and Mary's Future*

Mary and Joseph would live the rest of their lives in Nazareth, where they grew up. Everyone in town would know that the father of Jesus was not Joseph and suspect Mary of being an adulteress. She would always be a person of bad character. She may not have had friends.

CULTURAL CUE: *Mary's Possible Future*

If she had been dismissed "quietly" (Matt. 1:19), Mary would have had few options. If her family let her stay with them, she could raise her child and bring great shame on her family. If they didn't let her stay, she would probably become a prostitute or be sold into slavery. Her child would have no credible future.

Questions to Help You Enter the Story

Write a sentence or two in response to these questions:

1. What might have been Mary's thoughts and feelings about (pick one):

   - Joseph's finding out that she was pregnant?
   - Joseph's plans to "dismiss her quietly" (Matt. 1:19)?
   - Joseph's having the dream and being told to marry her?

2. Once Joseph agreed to take Mary as his wife, how might they have related to each other in a positive way?

   - Bearing social and cultural scorn together as well as being part of God's plan might have bonded them.
   - They could have shared what it was like to have an angel speak to them, and experienced further bonding. Neither had to question their sanity over having seen an angel.

- Perhaps Mary felt she was now part of a "team" in God's adventure.
- Other:

Responding to the Story

Read the passage aloud to yourself slowly. Try to picture yourself observing Mary, or even put yourself in her place, seeing what she saw and feeling what she may have felt.

- What do I (as Mary or observing Mary) hear or see?
- What word, phrase, scene, or image emerges from the scripture and stays with me?
- What feelings do I imagine Mary had that resonate with me?

Perhaps God is offering you an invitation in this passage to enlarge your understanding in the next few days. In what way might that be? Sit quietly for a few minutes, pondering these questions:

- How is my life touched today by this passage?
- Is there some idea, feeling, or intention I need to embrace from it? If so, what?
- What might God be inviting me to be or know or understand or feel or even do?

Take a few minutes to respond to God about this in prayer.

- What do I most want to say to God about this experience in scripture?

You might want to write your prayer in the space below.

Sit in the quiet and consider:

- How did God (or God's actions) seem to me in this passage? What does this tell me about what God is like?

Spend a few minutes simply resting in God's presence. Finish by reciting the prayer of Ignatius on page 22.

Day 3
Joseph's Parents' Point of View
(Matthew 1:18-25)

Settling In

Quiet yourself. Get in a relaxed position. Breathe in and out slowly a few times.

Pray the opening prayer on page 13.

Entering the Story

Read the passage (Matt. 1:18-25) on page 64 above silently. Then read the notes that follow the scripture text and the Cues above as well as this Cultural Cue. This time think about how Joseph's parents might have experienced Joseph's dream and decision not to divorce her.

CULTURAL CUE: *Joseph's Parents' Predicament*

For a family in these times, a son was the pride and joy. Joseph's parents, if alive, would have been deeply affected by his decision. If he had divorced Mary quietly, they would have been shamed because although their son did nothing wrong, he had made a bad choice for a wife. As it stood, their son was married to an adulteress who clearly should have been stoned, but was not.

Fathers and sons usually worked together. So Joseph's father and brothers would have been his coworkers. That could have been helpful, or it could have been awkward.

CULTURAL CUE: *Joseph's Parents' Possible Choices*

Below are three possible circumstances under which Joseph might have lived. Read each one and then write a sentence or two in response to the questions that follow.

Disapproval: Let's say Joseph's parents disapproved of Joseph's choosing to wed Mary. If so, they probably would never have spoken to her. In fact, Joseph and Mary would possibly never be welcomed in their home. Yet they still would have been neighbors in the small village of Nazareth (population: approximately four hundred[6]). They would have seen one another (as well as their grandchildren) many times. Would they interact? Could Joseph still work in the family carpentry "company," or would he have to fend for himself?

Immediate acceptance: If Joseph's parents immediately accepted his decision, they would have experienced the derision of friends. Perhaps when Joseph and his sons (and possibly his father and brothers) walked to Sepphoris (about an hour away by foot[7]) to work, no one would walk with them. Perhaps Joseph and his sons would have been left out of lucrative work projects. Perhaps people wouldn't hire them for personal carpentry projects even in Nazareth.

Eventual acceptance: Estrangement might have lasted for a while, but Joseph's parents might have eventually renewed their relationship with the couple and their children. Perhaps seeing their own grandchildren playing in the village would have won them over. Throughout the entire time, they would have experienced derision and isolation from neighbors.

1. If Joseph's parents disapproved, what might have been their thoughts and feelings? What might have been Joseph's thoughts and feelings?

2. If Joseph's parents immediately accepted Joseph's decision (as well as Mary), what might have been their thoughts and feelings? What might have been Joseph's thoughts and feelings?

3. If Joseph's parents eventually accepted the circumstances, what might have been their thoughts and feelings? What might have been Joseph's thoughts and feelings?

Responding to the Story

Read the passage aloud again. Imagine yourself in Joseph's parents' place. Consider their emotional state, but also their (lack of) social status in the community. Or see yourself as their relative, or an observer in town, seeing what they saw and feeling what they may have felt.

- What do I (as Joseph or observing Joseph) hear or see?
- What word, phrase, scene, or image emerges from the scripture and stays with me?
- What feelings do I imagine his parents had that resonate with me?

Perhaps God is offering you an invitation in this passage to enlarge your understanding in the next few days. In what way might that be? Sit quietly for a few minutes, pondering these questions:

- How is my life touched today by this passage?
- Is there some idea, feeling, or intention I need to embrace from it? If so, what?
- What might God be inviting me to be or know or understand or feel or even do?

Take a few minutes to respond to God about this in prayer.

■ What do I most want to say to God about this experience in scripture?

You might want to write your prayer in the space below.

Sit in the quiet and consider:

■ How did God (or God's actions) seem to me in this passage? What does this tell me about what God is like?

Spend a few minutes simply resting in God's presence. Finish by reciting the prayer of Ignatius on page 22.

Day 4
Mary's Parents' Point of View
(Matthew 1:18-25)

Settling In

Quiet yourself. Get in a relaxed position. Breathe in and out slowly a few times.

Pray the opening prayer on page 13.

Entering the Story

Read the passage (Matt. 1:18-25) on page 64 above silently. Then read the notes that follow the scripture text and Cultural Cues above. Read also the Cue below. Consider this time how Mary's parents might have experienced first Mary's pregnancy and then Joseph's dream and decision not to divorce her.

CULTURAL CUE: *Mary's Parents' Predicament*

For a short time, Mary's parents no doubt lived in the fear that their daughter would be stoned for adultery. Their agony may have subsided somewhat as they saw that she would live and even be married, although she would live in shame her entire life.

So Mary's parents would also live in shame. Perhaps whatever Mary's father did for a living was now not possible because no one would interact with him (buy from him or hire him to work). They would have experienced financial as well as social pressures.

Questions to Help You Enter the Story

Pick an answer or answers to the questions below or write a sentence or two in response:

1. What might have been Mary's parents' thoughts when they found out Mary was pregnant?

    ■ Shame that they had raised a daughter who was immoral; feelings of inadequacy for having raised a daughter who became pregnant before she was married.

    ■ Puzzlement by her explanations: She's seen an angel. The angel told her that the "power of the Most High will overshadow you."

    ■ Perhaps one parent believed her and the other did not. So they were divided and the household was tense.

    ■ Other:

2. What might have been their thoughts when Joseph decided to marry her?

    ■ Relief. She would not die. Their grandchild would not die.

    ■ Fear for their daughter's future, for the future of their grandchild.

    ■ Other:

Responding to the Story

Read the passage aloud again. Imagine yourself in Mary's parents' places, seeing what they saw and feeling what they may have felt. Or imagine yourself observing them as a close friend or relative. Consider their emotional states but also their (lack of) social status in the community.

- What do I (as Mary's parents or observing Mary's parents) hear or see?
- What word, phrase, scene, or image emerges from the scripture and stays with me?
- What feelings do I imagine Mary's parents had that resonate with me?

Perhaps God is offering you an invitation in this passage to enlarge your understanding in the next few days. In what way might that be? Sit quietly for a few minutes, pondering these questions:

- How is my life touched today by this passage?
- Is there some idea, feeling, or intention I need to embrace from it? If so, what?
- What might God be inviting me to be or know or understand or feel or even do?

Take a few minutes to respond to God about this in prayer.

- What do I most want to say to God about this experience in scripture?

You might want to write your prayer down below.

Sit in the quiet and consider:

- How did God (or God's actions) seem to me in this passage? What does this tell me about what God is like?

Spend a few minutes simply resting in God's presence. Close by reciting the prayer of Ignatius on page 22.

Day 5
How the People of Nazareth Regard "the Scandal"
(Matthew 1:18-25)

Settling In

Quiet yourself. Breathe in and out slowly a few times.
 Pray the opening prayer on page 13.

Entering the Story

Read the passage (Matt. 1:18-25) on page 64 above silently. Then read the notes that follow the scripture text and Cultural Cue above. Read also the Cue below. Consider this time how the people of Nazareth might have experienced Mary's pregnancy and Joseph's response.

CULTURAL CUE: *Nazareth*

This town of perhaps four hundred is not located in the much more pious region of Judea. Instead, it's located in Galilee, miles away from Jerusalem, the Holy City. The great trade routes of the world came through Galilee, bringing all kinds of outside influences. Just four miles away was King Herod's capital city of Sepphoris, the "ornament of all Galilee."[8] "Jesus lived in a Galilean culture much more urban and sophisticated,"[9] more cosmopolitan, than some have thought it to be. Yet Nazareth itself was of little consequence. As Nathanael huffed, "Can anything good come out of Nazareth?" (John 1:46).

 So Nazareth might have had some "worldly" citizens who would have accepted Mary and her son. At least some people liked Jesus: "Jesus increased in wisdom and in years, and in divine and human favor" (Luke 2:52). According to custom, Jesus would have been a teacher in the sabbath school and eventually the CEO of Joseph and Sons Construction Company after Joseph died. Perhaps people grew to like him through their business dealings with him. Perhaps they had heard about how he had startled and amazed the teachers of the Temple when he stayed behind (Luke 2:41-51). Eventually, however, they did reject Jesus and even tried to kill him (Matt. 13:54-58; Mark 6:1-6; Luke 4:28-30). Even then, Jesus was "amazed at their unbelief" (Mark 6:6).

Questions to Help You Enter the Story

Write a sentence or two in response to these questions:

1. As you move into this scene in a few minutes and try to picture the Nazareth townspeople or put yourself in their place, you might consider the variety of people likely present:

   - Those who never accepted Jesus, remembering Mary's pregnancy and being suspicious. Perhaps they never associated with Joseph or Mary.
   - Those who didn't know what to think about Jesus' parentage, but accepted Joseph, Mary, and Jesus anyway.

   What other ideas might people of Nazareth had?

2. If I had been a friend or a coworker of Joseph, how might I have responded? With anger? Disappointment? Compassion?

3. What sort of behavior makes it difficult for me to accept people? Am I more accepting—or less accepting—during the holidays? Why do I think that is?

Responding to the Story

Read the passage aloud again. Imagine yourself observing the people in Nazareth and how they treated Mary and her parents and Joseph and his parents. What sort of gossip did they perhaps hear? Consider their struggle with what was just according to the legalistic views (Mary should have been stoned) versus Joseph's "justice" of reprocessing anger into grace.

- What do I (as Joseph's parents or observing Joseph's parents) hear or see?
- What word, phrase, scene, or image emerges from the scripture and stays with me?
- What feelings do I imagine the people of Nazareth had that resonate with me?

Perhaps God is offering you an invitation in this passage to enlarge your understanding in the next few days. In what way might that be? Sit quietly for a few minutes, pondering these questions:

- How is my life touched today by this passage?
- Is there some idea, feeling, or intention I need to embrace from it? If so, what?
- What might God be inviting me to be or know or understand or feel or even do?

Take a few minutes to respond to God about this in prayer.

- What do I most want to say to God about this experience in scripture?

You might want to write your prayer in the space below.

Sit in the quiet and consider:

- How did God (or God's actions) seem to me in this passage? What does this tell me about what God is like?

Spend a few minutes simply resting in God's presence. Finish by reciting the prayer of Ignatius on page 22.

Day 6
How Mary Sees Herself
(Luke 1:46-55)

Settling In

Quiet yourself. Breathe in and out slowly a few times.
     Pray the opening prayer on page 13.

Entering the Story

Read the passage (Luke 1:46-55) below silently. Then read the
notes in the right-hand column. Read the passage to yourself aloud,
slowly. Consider how the notes affect your experience of the story.

LUKE 1:46-55	OTHERS' VIEWS OF MARY
46And Mary said,	immoral
"My soul magnifies the Lord,	deserving to die
47 and my spirit rejoices in God my Savior,	getting off easy
48 for he has looked with favor on the lowliness of his servant.	without God's blessing
Surely, from now on all generations will call me blessed;	no future and no future for her children
49 for the Mighty One has done great things for me, and holy is his name.	
50 His mercy is for those who fear him from generation to generation.	
51 He has shown strength with his arm; he has scattered the proud in the thoughts of their hearts.	
52 He has brought down the power- ful from their thrones,	

and lifted up the lowly;
53 he has filled the hungry with
   good things,
   and sent the rich away empty.
54 He has helped his servant Israel,
   in remembrance of his mercy,
55 according to the promise he
   made to our ancestors,
   to Abraham and to his descen-
   dants forever."

Questions to Help You Enter the Story

Write a sentence or two in response to these questions:

1. While the townspeople of Nazareth no doubt looked down on Mary, and perhaps even hated her, how did she view herself (based on the Magnificat)?

2. In what circumstances do people view me very differently from the way I see myself in relation to God (my "magnificat view" of myself)? What feelings and attitudes did Mary have that I want now for myself?

Keep in mind everything we've meditated on this week:

- Joseph the Just might have been very angry, but he reprocessed his anger into grace, becoming restorative instead of accusative.
- Mary may have been hesitant or fearful about her future with Joseph even after he decided to marry her.
- Joseph's parents may have been very conflicted about what to think of Mary. How could she be an adulteress?

- Mary's parents would be shunned the rest of their lives. How would they now relate to their daughter?
- Some in the little town of Nazareth might have been quite gossipy about Mary while others may have taken what they considered a "broader" or more "liberal" view, due to the culture in the wider and more sophisticated world of Sepphoris and Galilee in general.

Responding to the Story

Read the passage aloud again. Imagine yourself in Mary's place, viewing herself a certain way while others scorned her. Consider her physical and emotional state. Or put yourself in Joseph's place, a just man viewing Mary very differently than his world and loved ones probably did. Imagine what either saw or felt about what they believed to be reality (as expressed in the Magnificat) versus what the culture around them said was reality.

- What do I (as Joseph or Mary) hear or see?
- What feelings do I imagine Mary or Joseph had that resonate with me?
- What word, phrase, scene, or image emerges from the scripture and stays with me?

Perhaps God is offering you an invitation in this passage to enlarge your understanding in the next few days. In what way might that be? Sit quietly for a few minutes, pondering these questions:

- How is my life touched today by this passage?
- Is there some idea, feeling, or intention I need to embrace from it? If so, what?
- What might God be inviting me to be or know or understand or feel or even do?

Take a few minutes to respond to God about this in prayer.

What do I most want to say to God about this experience in scripture?

You might want to write your prayer in the space below.

Sit in the quiet and consider:

How did God (or God's actions) seem to me in this passage? What does this tell me about what God is like?

Spend a few minutes simply resting in God's presence. Finish by reciting the prayer of Ignatius on page 22.

Day 7
Take Two

Settling In

Quiet yourself as in the group experience. Get in a relaxed position. Breathe in and out slowly a few times.

Pray the opening prayer on page 13.

Entering the Story

Think back over this week's meditations. Which one would you like to experience again? Maybe it was the one you seemed to resonate with the most. Or perhaps it was one you liked or understood the least, and you'd like to try it again now that you've done a few more meditations.

Meditations to choose from in Week 3, Experiencing Joseph's Challenge, are

- Day 1: Joseph "the Just" and His Dreams (Matthew 1:18-25), page 63.

- Day 2: Mary Experiences Joseph's Decisions (possibilities of bonding), page 69.
- Day 3: Joseph's Parents' Point of View (deciding how to interact with Joseph, Mary, and their grandson), page 72.
- Day 4: Mary's Parents' Point of View (deciding how to interact with Joseph, Mary, and their grandson; bearing up to Nazareth's scorn), page 75.
- Day 5: How the People of Nazareth Regard "the Scandal" (Some might have been outraged while others more tolerant), page 78.
- Day 6: How Mary Sees Herself (Luke 1:46-55), page 81.

EXPERIENCING THE BIRTH OF CHRIST

Fourth Sunday of Advent
Mary Gives Birth
(Luke 2:1-7)
(Possible Christmas Eve or Christmas Day Meditation)

Opening Ourselves *(10 minutes)*

Take a few deep breaths. Pray this opening prayer together:

> Let us release the cares of our day,
> and open our eyes to the wonder of God.
> With an attitude of empathy to people of another time,
> let us open our hearts and minds to God.
> Let us prepare to experience God's word to us
> through the presence of the Holy Spirit.

Entering the Story *(20 minutes)*

Read the passage below (Luke 2:1-7) silently. The leader will then read the notes that follow the scripture text. Consider how they affect the story. Then close your eyes and listen as a group member reads the passage.

LUKE 2:1-7

[1]In those days a decree went out from **Emperor Augustus** that all the world should be **registered**. [2]This was the first registration and was taken while Quirinius was governor of Syria. [3]All went to **their own towns** to be registered. [4]Joseph also went from the town of Nazareth in Galilee to Judea, to the city of David called **Bethlehem**, because he was descended from the house and family of David.

[5]He went to be registered with Mary, to whom he was engaged and who was expecting a child. [6]While they were there, the time came for her to deliver her child. [7]And she gave birth to her firstborn son and wrapped him in **bands of cloth**, and laid him in a **manger**, because there was no place for them in the inn.

Italicized Words & Phrases

Emperor Augustus . . . registered Augustus was the Roman emperor and he ordered that everyone within the empire be counted in a census. Perhaps Luke wanted us to see the early contrast between one of the most powerful kingdoms the world has known (Rome) and the everlasting kingdom of God.

their own towns the towns in which their ancestors originally lived.

Bethlehem A town located a few miles from Jerusalem in Judea. This was King David's hometown. Micah the prophet spoke of it: "O Bethlehem . . . from you shall come forth for me one who is to rule in Israel, whose origin is from of old, from ancient days" (5:2).

bands of cloth kept a baby feeling snug, as if in the mother's womb.

manger feeding trough for animals

HISTORICAL AND CULTURAL CUE: *Setting*

Scholars have been puzzled about why Joseph and Mary were supposedly turned away from all homes and even an inn in Bethlehem when hospitality was a nonnegotiable requirement in the Middle East at that time. Joseph would have had many relatives in Bethlehem to welcome them, and even nonrelatives would have welcomed him as Davidic royalty because he was a Bethlehemite. Here's an explanation: "For more than a hundred years scholars resident in the Middle East have understood Luke 2:7 as referring to a family room with mangers cut into the floor at one end."[1] Simple village homes in Palestine had two rooms. One was exclusively for guests (the upper room or "prophet's chamber"). The other room was the main room where the entire family cooked, ate, slept, and lived. At the end of that room by the door was a small area that was lower and cordoned off by timber. Into that area each night were brought the family cow, donkey, and a few sheep. (Animals kept the house warm and they were kept safe inside.) Every morning the animals were taken out and the stall cleaned.[2] Scholars surmise the "inn" (*katalyma*) was probably that guest room. (This may explain why the wise men visited the family in a "house" [Matt. 2:11].)

This would mean that Joseph and Mary were graciously accepted into the main room with the family because the "inn" or guest room was full. In that main room would have been a manger for the animals that stayed there at night.[3]

HISTORICAL CUE: *The Journey*

People usually traveled in caravans with other people. This was safer in case of accident or injury or possible attack by bandits, as well as being more enjoyable. With a census like this involving as many people as it did, a caravan going to Bethlehem would not be hard to find or join. Caravans would travel about twenty miles in a day, and the distance between Nazareth and Bethlehem (eighty miles) would translate into a four-day journey.[4]

Questions to Help You Enter the Story

Write a sentence or two in response to these questions:

1. Mary and Joseph had to trust God for many things in their travel (probably with strangers) for four days to a city they may or may not have visited before. List some of these concerns.

   ■ How they would be received by their hosts if they knew about Mary's pregnancy occurring before the marriage.
   ■ Other:
   ■ Other:

- Other:
- Other:
- Other:

2. What might Mary have been thinking and feeling as she stared at the baby she had just given birth to? (If you wish to review Gabriel's words to her, read Luke 1:30-33.)

3. What did Mary probably learn or know in this experience?

Responding to the Story *(15 minutes)*

As the leader reads the passage aloud, try to picture Mary and imagine her facial expression as she cares for her little one. Or imagine yourself observing her, seeing what she saw and feeling what she might have felt. If you wish, you can lie on the floor or prop your feet up on another chair.

- What do I (as Mary or observing Mary) hear or see?
- What word, phrase, scene, or image emerges from the scripture and stays with me?
- What feelings do I imagine Mary had?

Perhaps God is offering you an invitation in this passage to enlarge your understanding in the next few days. In what way might that be?

Sit quietly for a few minutes, pondering these questions:

- How is my life touched today by this passage?
- Is there some idea, feeling, or intention I need to embrace from it? If so, what?
- What might God be inviting me to be or know or understand or feel or even do?

Be open to the quiet, but don't feel pressured to come up with an answer. Use this space to write anything you wish to:

Take a few minutes to respond to God about this in prayer.

- What do I most want to say to God about this experience in scripture?

Sit in the quiet and consider:

- How did God (or God's actions) seem to me in this passage? What does this tell me about what God is like?

Spend a few minutes simply resting in God's presence.

Group Sharing (10 minutes)

If you wish, share what you think God might have been saying to you, inviting you to be or know or understand or feel or even do. If you don't wish to speak, listen to the others. You may find that what they say relates to you. It's also interesting to see how God speaks to our sisters and brothers in Christ differently than God speak to us.

Closing Prayer (5 minutes)

Grant us wisdom and courage this week:
to trust you to provide what we need just when we need it;
to taste and see your presence in new ways;
to trust that you will do good and joyful things in our lives and in the world.

During the Week

Before going to bed or when you're doing a relatively simple chore (such as, taking out trash, washing dishes, locking doors before retiring), reflect on this:

- Is there anything God might be leading me to do because of what came to me today in this passage?

This must not be forced or contrived or according to the usual tapes that might play in your mind (for example, fix this person; make someone happy; correct people's thinking; strive a little harder). God may not be leading you to do anything; but if so, be open to what that might be.

Project: Ask God to show you someone on a kind of journey. How might you help that person with practical details? With emotions? With trusting God?

Day 2
Joseph Arranges the Bethlehem Journey
(Luke 2:1-7)
(Possible Christmas Eve or Christmas Day Meditation)

Settling In

Quiet yourself as in the group experience. Get in a relaxed position (as long as it won't allow you to fall asleep). Breathe in and out slowly a few times.

Place a bookmark at the beginning of Week One so you can refer to resources there. Pray the opening prayer on page 13.

Entering the Story

Read silently the passage (Luke 2:1-7) on page 88. Then read the notes that follow the scripture text. Think about how they affect the story. Then read the passage to yourself aloud slowly, taking into consideration all the comments below.

HISTORICAL AND BIBLICAL CUE: *Joseph's Relatives*

Joseph would have been much more familiar with the people in this host home than Mary was. Perhaps his family had visited them on one of the usual three-times-a-year visits to Jerusalem since Bethlehem is about six miles from Jerusalem.[5]

But we don't know how much their host family knew about their situation. According to the text, Mary and Joseph are still just engaged, yet Mary is giving birth (Luke 2:5-6). Recall that Joseph has been called "Joseph the Just" because of how he reprocessed probable anger (fuming, see Day 1, Week 3) into grace. But in this scene he had heavy responsibilities for transporting and taking care of Mary and the baby, so he might not have had time to concern himself with what his relatives thought of him.

Questions to Help You Enter the Story

Write a sentence or two in response to these questions:

1. How might Joseph have felt the same or different from any other first-time father?

2. What might Joseph have been thinking and feeling as he stared at the baby Mary held and as he remembered Gabriel's words that this baby would "save his people from their sins" (Matt. 1:21)?

Responding to the Story

Read the passage aloud again. Imagine yourself observing Joseph or even in Joseph's place. Consider his physical and emotional state. What might have been his facial expression?

- What did Joseph see and feel?
- What word, phrase, scene, or image emerges from the scripture and stays with me?
- What feelings do I imagine Joseph had that resonate with me?

Perhaps God is offering you an invitation in this passage to enlarge your understanding in the next few days. In what way might that be? Sit quietly for a few minutes, pondering these questions:

- How is my life touched today by this passage?
- Is there some idea, feeling, or intention I need to embrace from it? If so, what?
- What might God be inviting me to be or know or understand or feel or even do?

Take a few minutes to respond to God about this in prayer.

- What do I most want to say to God about this experience in scripture?

Sit in the quiet and consider:

- How did God (or God's actions) seem to me in this passage? What does this tell me about what God is like?

Spend a few minutes simply resting in God's presence. Finish by reciting the prayer of Ignatius on page 22.

Day 3
A Family Receives Mary and Joseph
(Luke 2:1-7)
(Possible Christmas Eve or Christmas Day Meditation)

Settling In

Quiet yourself. Get in a relaxed position. Breathe in and out slowly a few times.

Pray the opening prayer on page 13.

Entering the Story

Read silently the passage (Luke 2:1-7) on page 88. Then read the notes that follow the scripture text. Consider how they affect the story. Then read the passage to yourself aloud slowly, taking into consideration all the comments below. Notice especially the Historical and Cultural Cue: *Setting* from Day 1.

HISTORICAL, CULTURAL, AND PICTURING CUE: *Family Room Becomes Birthing Room*

The family that received Mary and Joseph (probably Joseph's relatives) graciously accepted Joseph and Mary into the main room with them because their guest room ("inn") was full. They also offered their animals' feeding trough (manger) as a handy crib.[6]

Imagine the village midwife arriving and the men leaving the main family room. Perhaps the young girls stayed to help. They may have sent the younger girls out to get fresh straw for the manger.

CONTEXTUAL CUE: *Future of Family Members*

Thirty years later, the younger members of this family may have encountered Jesus the many times he came to Jerusalem (just six miles away). Maybe they saw Jesus' healings there (the lame man at the pool), his cleansing of the Temple for God's use, or heard about the leaders' intentions to kill Jesus. They may have watched Jesus' triumphal entry into Jerusalem (Palm Sunday) and witnessed the trick questions he was asked about giving to Caesar or God. They may have even watched Jesus' crucifixion and been aware of his resurrection (or encountered him!). They probably also remembered his birth and perhaps had held him when he was a newborn.

Questions to Help You Enter the Story

Write a sentence or two in response to these questions:

1. This family would probably have known about Joseph and Mary's circumstances yet still welcomed them, even into their family room. What words describe such people?

2. When have I inconvenienced myself because I saw someone in a desperate situation? Was there anything about the experience that turned out to be especially joyful, inspiring, or fun?

Responding to the Story

Read the passage aloud again (Luke 2:1-7). Imagine yourself in the family's place. You might be the husband or the wife or an older child or perhaps a little one who barely understands what's going on. What do you think of this couple? Of this birth? How do you feel about welcoming them? What are you perhaps thinking in your mind but not saying aloud to anyone else?

Optional Idea: When doing this kind of participative meditation, some people find it easier to see themselves as inanimate objects or animals rather than as a person. This is not unusual. So you may perhaps find yourself being the house that sheltered the Holy Family or one of the animals that was probably present in the evening (although none are mentioned).

- What do I hear or see?
- What word, phrase, scene, or image emerges from the scripture and stays with me?
- What feelings do I imagine these family members had that resonate with me?

Perhaps God is offering you an invitation in this passage to enlarge your understanding in the next few days. In what way might that be? Sit quietly for a few minutes, pondering these questions:

- How is my life touched today by this passage?
- Is there some idea, feeling, or intention I need to embrace from it? If so, what?
- What might God be inviting me to be or know or understand or feel or even do?

Take a few minutes to respond to God about this in prayer.

- What do I most want to say to God about this experience in scripture?

Sit in the quiet and consider:

- How did God (or God's actions) seem to me in this passage? What does this tell me about what God is like?

Spend a few minutes simply resting in God's presence. Finish by reciting the prayer of Ignatius on page 22.

Day 4
The Family That Kept Them: Thirty Years Later
(Mark 10:13-16; Matthew 10:40-42)

Settling In

Quiet yourself. Get in a relaxed position. Breathe in and out slowly a few times.

Pray the opening prayer on page 13.

Entering the Story

Read silently the passage below (Mark 10:13-16; Matt. 10:40-42), imagining for a moment that you were a member of the household and are now in the crowd listening to Jesus teach. Hear what he says about the importance of receiving children and receiving prophets. Imagine that Jesus looked at you as he said these things.[7] You might want to also imagine that you are among the people who brought their children to him to be blessed. Also read the notes that follow the scripture text. Consider how they affect the story.

Then read the passage to yourself aloud slowly, and try to fully enter the situation.

Mark 10:13-16; Matthew 10:40-42

¹³People were bringing little children to him in order that he might **touch** them; and the disciples spoke sternly to them. ¹⁴But when Jesus saw this, he was indignant and said to them, "Let the little children come to me; do not stop them; for it is to such as these that the **kingdom of God** belongs. ¹⁵Truly I tell you, whoever does not **receive the kingdom**

Italicized Words & Phrases

touch lay hands on them and bless them.

kingdom of God The kingdom is future but is also present. Jesus said, "The "the kingdom of God is within you" (Luke 17:21, KJV). We can live in and experience kingdom life now.

of God as a little child will never enter it." ¹⁶And he took them up in his arms, laid his hands on them, and blessed them. . . .

⁴⁰"Whoever welcomes you welcomes me, and whoever welcomes me welcomes the one who sent me. ⁴¹Whoever **welcomes a prophet** in the name of a prophet will receive a prophet's reward; and whoever welcomes a righteous person in the name of a righteous person will receive the reward of the righteous; ⁴²and whoever gives even a cup of cold water to one of these little ones in the name of a disciple—truly I tell you, none of these will lose their reward."

---

welcomes a prophet Prophets weren't always welcomed; Israel's royalty hunted down Elijah, and King Ahab called him a "troubler of Israel" (1 Kings 18:17). However, the Palestinian widow of Zarephath welcomed him, and he later blessed her by saving her son's life (1 Kings 17:8-24).

CULTURAL CUE: *Family Customs*

As you do this exercise, you may see yourself as a small child when your family received Joseph, Mary, and Jesus. That might suggest you wouldn't have been aware of what your family did. But in ancient Middle Eastern culture, the family unit had one identity. If your family did it, you did it. If your family did it in the past, you most likely would do it again because this was what your family was like. It was your family's custom to welcome even outcasts and lawbreakers.

Questions to Help You Enter the Story

Write a sentence or two in response to these questions:

1. Based on what you know about the character of Jesus, what look might have been on his face as he said this in the crowd and caught your eye: "Whoever welcomes me . . . whoever welcomes a prophet . . . whoever gives a cup of cold water" (Matt. 10:40-42)? Why?

2. How might I feel now that Jesus has become a famous but controversial prophet? How might I feel when hearing about the Crucifixion? The Resurrection?

3. In my contemporary context, what does it mean to be a welcoming person? One who *receives* others?

Responding to the Story

Read the passage aloud again. Imagine yourself observing someone from the hosting family hearing Jesus' words. Or put yourself in the place of someone from that hosting family, perhaps as an old man or woman, or as an adult in their thirties who was a small child when the Holy Family came. Imagine yourself receiving Jesus' words, as your family received the Holy Family.

- What do I hear or see?
- What word, phrase, scene, or image emerges from the scripture and stays with me?
- What feelings do I imagine some of these now-grown children had that resonate with me?

Perhaps God is offering you an invitation in this passage to enlarge your understanding in the next few days. In what way might that be? Sit quietly for a few minutes, pondering these questions:

- How is my life touched today by this passage?
- Is there some idea, feeling, or intention I need to embrace from it? If so, what?
- What might God be inviting me to be or know or understand or feel or even do?

Take a few minutes to respond to God about this in prayer.

■   What do I most want to say to God about this experience in
    scripture?

Sit in the quiet and consider:

■   How did God (or God's actions) seem to me in this passage?
    What does this tell me about what God is like?

Spend a few minutes simply resting in God's presence.
Finish by reciting the prayer of Ignatius on page 22.

Day 5
The Shepherds' Mission
(Luke 2:8-20)
(Possible Christmas Eve or Christmas Day Meditation)

Settling In

Quiet yourself as in the group experience. Get in a relaxed position. Breathe in and out slowly a few times.
    Pray the opening prayer on page 13.

Entering the Story

Read the passage (Luke 2:8-20) below silently. Then read the notes
that follow the scripture text. Think about how they affect the

story. Then read the passage to yourself aloud slowly, taking into consideration all the comments below.

LUKE 2:8-20

[8]In that region there were shepherds living in the fields, keeping watch over their flock by night. [9]Then an angel of the Lord stood before them, and the glory of the Lord shone around them, and they were **terrified**. [10]But the angel said to them, "Do not be afraid; for see—I am bringing you good news of great joy for all the people: [11]to you is born this day in the city of David a Savior, who is the Messiah, the Lord. [12]This will be a sign for you: you will find a child **wrapped in bands of cloth** and lying in a **manger**."

[13]And suddenly there was with the angel a multitude of the heavenly host, praising God and saying,

[14] "Glory to God in the highest heaven,
and on earth peace among those whom he favors!"

[15]When the angels had left them and gone into heaven, the shepherds said to one another, "Let us go now to Bethlehem and see this thing that has taken place, which the Lord has made known to us."

[16]So they went with haste and found Mary and Joseph, and the child lying in the **manger**. [17]When they saw this, they made known what had been told them about this child; [18]and all who heard it were amazed at what the shepherds told them.

[19]But Mary treasured all these words and **pondered** them in her heart. [20]The shepherds returned, glorifying and praising God for all they had heard and seen, as it had been told them.

Italicized Words & Phrases

terrified no doubt by the appearance of angels, and an angel of the Lord speaking to them.

wrapped in bands of cloth to keep a baby feeling snug, as if in the mother's womb.

Manger is mentioned three times in Luke 2 because it's the shepherds' clue that they've found the right baby (vv. 7, 12, 16).

pondered It has been said that we don't learn from experience but from reflecting on that experience.[8] Mary reflected well.

HISTORICAL CUE: *Socioeconomic Level of Shepherds*

"Shepherds in first century Palestine were poor, and rabbinic traditions label them as unclean." They were considered "lowly, uneducated types," who were "close to the bottom of the social scale in their society."[9]

HISTORICAL CUE: *Why an Angelic Chorus Was Needed*

From the shepherds' point of view, the parents of a child who was truly the Messiah would reject them because of their own low social status. How could shepherds be convinced to expect a welcome if they visited this family?

The angels seemed to anticipate the shepherds' anxiety and told the shepherds they would find the baby wrapped in bands of cloth. This assured their welcome because peasants, like shepherds, wrapped newborns in bands of cloth. That would provide a clue to the shepherds that they were not social inferiors to these parents.

Furthermore, the angels alerted the shepherds that they would find the baby lying in an animals' food trough. This information told them they would find the Christ child in an ordinary peasant home such as theirs. He was not in a governor's mansion or a wealthy merchant's guest room but in a simple two-room house like theirs. This was *really* good news.[10] So they would not be told, "Unclean shepherds—be gone!" Bands of cloth and a feeding trough as a cradle were true and good signs for lowly shepherds.

PICTURING AND HISTORICAL CUE: *A Variety of Shepherds*

When you picture the shepherds, consider that they varied in age. Some might have been older, but often young teenage boys were shepherds. Perhaps some still doubted and others were obviously fearful. (The angels told them, "Do not be afraid.")

PICTURING CUE: *What the Shepherds Saw*

All "of a sudden came the long-delayed, unthought-of announcement. Heaven and earth seemed to mingle, as suddenly an Angel stood before their dazzled eyes, while the outstreaming glory of the Lord seemed to enwrap them, as in a mantle of light. Surprise, awe, fear would be hushed into calm and expectancy."[11]

Questions to Help You Enter the Story

Write a sentence or two in response to these questions:

1. Look at the above Picturing Cue: *What the Shepherds Saw* and underline the words that most help you enter the scene, to think of what it might have been like for the shepherds.

2. How might shepherds have felt at being honored this way— able to view the Messiah child?

3. What might Mary have thought about the arrival of such lowly people as shepherds, in light of her song (God had "lifted up the lowly" [Luke 1:52])?

Responding to the Story

Read the passage aloud again. Imagine yourself as a shepherd of any age (choose an age or see what comes to you). Consider your lack of social status and perhaps sleepy state. Picture the look on this person's face or put yourself in his or her place.

- What do I (as a shepherd) hear or see? Or what do I see as I observe the shepherds?
- What word, phrase, scene, or image emerges from the scripture and stays with me?
- What feelings do I imagine some of the shepherds had that resonate with me?

Perhaps God is offering you an invitation in this passage to enlarge your understanding in the next few days. In what way might that be? Sit quietly for a few minutes, pondering these questions:

- How is my life touched today by this passage?
- Is there some idea, feeling, or intention I need to embrace from it? If so, what?
- What might God be inviting me to be or know or understand or feel or even do?

Take a few minutes to respond to God about this in prayer.

- What do I most want to say to God about this experience in scripture?

Sit in the quiet and consider:

- How did God (or God's actions) seem to me in this passage? What does this tell me about what God is like?

Spend a few minutes simply resting in God's presence. Finish by reciting the prayer of Ignatius on page 22.

Day 6
Simeon and Anna Celebrate
(Luke 2:21-38)

Settling In

Quiet yourself and breathe in and out slowly a few times.
    Pray the opening prayer on page 13.

Entering the Story

Read the passage (Luke 2:21-38) below silently. Then read the notes that follow the scripture text. Think about how these details affect the story. Then read the passage to yourself aloud slowly, taking into consideration all the comments below.

LUKE 2:21-38

²¹After eight days had passed, it was **time to circumcise** the child; and he was called Jesus, the name given by the angel before he was conceived in the womb.

²²When the time came for **their purification** according to the law of Moses, they brought him up to Jerusalem to **present him to the Lord** ²³(as it is written in the law of the Lord, "Every firstborn male shall be designated as holy to the Lord"), ²⁴and they offered a sacrifice according to what is stated in the law of the Lord, "a **pair of turtledoves or two young pigeons**."

²⁵Now there was a man in Jerusalem whose name was Simeon; this man was righteous and devout, looking forward to the consolation of Israel, and the Holy Spirit rested on him.

²⁶It had been revealed to him by the Holy Spirit that he would not see death before he had seen the Lord's Messiah.

²⁷Guided by the Spirit, Simeon came into the temple; and when the parents brought in the child Jesus, to do for him what was customary under the law, ²⁸Simeon took him in his arms and praised God, saying,

²⁹ "Master, now you are dismissing your servant in peace,
according to your word;
³⁰ for my eyes have seen your **salvation**,
³¹ which you have prepared in the presence of all peoples,

Italicized Words & Phrases

time to circumcise This special ceremony always occurred on the eighth day in the home and then the child was named.

their purification A woman was considered impure for 40 days after childbirth (Lev. 12).

present him to the Lord As the firstborn son, Jesus was consecrated to the service of God.[12]

pair of turtledoves or two young pigeons Mary and Joseph's purification sacrifice was not a lamb (as the rich offered) but these birds, the offering of poorer people.[13]

salvation deliverance from danger in this life; healing and spiritual and eternal deliverance in the next life.

³² a *light for revelation to the Gentiles*
and for glory to your people Israel."

³³And the child's father and mother were amazed at what was being said about him. ³⁴Then Simeon blessed them and said to his mother Mary, "This child is destined for the falling and the rising of many in Israel, and to be a sign that will be opposed ³⁵so that the inner thoughts of many will be revealed—and a sword will pierce your own soul too."

³⁶There was also a prophet, **Anna** the daughter of Phanuel, of the tribe of Asher. She was of a great age, having lived with her husband seven years after her marriage, ³⁷then as a widow to the age of eighty-four. She never left the temple but worshiped there with fasting and prayer night and day. ³⁸At that moment she came, and began to praise God and to speak about the child to all who were looking for the redemption of Jerusalem.

light for revelation to the Gentiles Simeon made this radical statement apparently before the Gentile magi had arrived.

Anna Although her words are not recorded, Luke characteristically includes female and well as male characters.

CHARACTER CUE: *Simeon's Character*

This deeply good and devout man lived in the prayerful expectancy that Israel would be delivered from its oppression. The Spirit rested on him (Luke 2:25); revealed truth to him (2:26); and guided him (2:27). Simeon's actions tell us a great deal about his personality: he took the baby Jesus in his arms; he expressed extreme gratefulness to God; and he blessed the couple that many people were probably not blessing. He also spoke directly to Mary, describing Jesus' future and how she needed to be prepared for pain. Keep in mind that men did not speak freely to women in public, but Simeon did.

CULTURAL CUE: *Intergenerational Mix*

Joseph and Mary no doubt needed the encouragement of Simeon and Anna as two older, wiser followers of God. If the young couple experienced self-doubt, these wise words and actions would probably have been remembered and even cherished. Simeon's and Anna's needs were also met. They needed to see the Messiah and die with hope that redemption was coming. Being with the family and holding the baby may have been one of the most fulfilling moments of their lives.

Questions to Help You Enter the Story

Write a sentence or two in response to these questions:

1. How might Mary and Joseph felt to be approached by these two older and wiser people who seemed to inhabit the Temple in Jerusalem (the holiest building they knew about)?

2. Both Simeon and Anna expressed extreme gratefulness and praise to God. Older people may be unhappily conscious of age's diminishments and even crabby about aches and pains. What makes us grateful as we become older?

3. How am I experiencing the blessing of knowing people older than I who can bless me, warn me, and advise me? How am I experiencing the blessing of bold, younger people who dare to venture out?

Responding to the Story

Read the passage aloud again. Imagine yourself in Simeon's or Anna's place, or in the place of Mary and Joseph observing them, or as a person observing the circumstances. Consider the physical and emotional states of Simeon and Anna. Picture their facial expressions.

- What do I (as one of these characters) see and hear?
- What word, phrase, scene, or image emerges from the scripture and stays with me?
- What feelings do I imagine one of these people had that resonate with me?

Perhaps God is offering you an invitation in this passage to enlarge your understanding. In what way might that be? Sit quietly for a few minutes, pondering these questions:

- How is my life touched today by this passage?
- Is there some idea, feeling, or intention I need to embrace from it? If so, what?
- What might God be inviting me to be or know or understand or feel or even do?

Take a few minutes to respond to God about this in prayer.

- What do I most want to say to God about this experience in scripture?

Sit in the quiet and consider:

- How did God (or God's actions) seem to me in this passage? What does this tell me about what God is like?

Spend a few minutes simply resting in God's presence. Finish by reciting the prayer of Ignatius on page 22.

Day 7
Wise Men Come
(Matthew 2:1-12)

Settling In

Quiet yourself as in the group experience. Breathe in and out slowly a few times.

Pray the opening prayer on page 13.

Entering The Story

Read the session passage (Matt. 2:1-12) silently. Then read the notes that follow the scripture text. Think about how they affect the story. Then read the passage to yourself aloud slowly, taking into consideration all the comments on the scripture.

Matthew 2:1-12

¹In the time of King Herod, after Jesus was born in Bethlehem of Judea, wise men *from the East* came to Jerusalem, ²asking, "Where is the child who has been born king of the Jews? For we observed *his star at its rising*, and have come to pay him homage." ³When King Herod heard this, he was frightened, and all Jerusalem with him; ⁴and calling together all the chief priests and scribes of the people, he inquired of them where the Messiah was to be born. ⁵They told him, "In Bethlehem of Judea; for so it has been written by the prophet:

⁶ 'And you, Bethlehem, in the land of Judah,
are by no means least among the rulers of Judah;

Italicized Words & Phrases

from the East Most likely these men came from Arabia.

his star at its rising This could have been Halley's Comet, a supernova, or the conjunction of Jupiter and Saturn, all of which occurred close to this time.[14]

for from you shall come a ruler
who is to shepherd my people Israel.'"
    [7]Then Herod secretly called for the wise men and learned from them
the exact time when the star had appeared. [8]Then he sent them to Bethlehem, saying, "Go and search diligently for the child; and when you have
found him, bring me word so that I may also go and pay him homage."
    [9]When they had heard the king, they set out; and there, ahead of
them, went the star that they had seen at its rising, until it stopped over
the place where the child was. [10]When they saw that the star had stopped,
they were overwhelmed with joy. [11]On entering the house, they saw the
child with Mary his mother; and they knelt down and paid him homage.
Then, opening their treasure chests, they offered him gifts of **gold, frankincense, and myrrh**. [12]And having been warned in a dream not to return
to Herod, they left for their own country by another road.

---

gold, frankincense, and myrrh Gold was mined in Arabia. Frankincense and
myrrh are harvested from trees that grow only in southern Arabia.[15] There
were three gifts, but there may have been only two men or many wise men.

HISTORICAL CUE: *Why Were Herod and Jerusalem Frightened?*

Herod was easily threatened in his kingship because he was not
truly a Jew. He was part Idumean (of an Arab tribe, Idumea)
through his father. His mother was from Petra, an Arab kingdom.
He was a Jew only religiously, and that because Idumeans had con-
verted only when forced. Culturally Herod was Greek, and politi-
cally Herod was Roman. So he was not secure in his throne, and he
quickly executed anyone he saw as a threat.[16]

    All Jerusalem may have been frightened because a so-called
king might cause an insurrection and bring the military might of
Rome down on them in full force. To keep the peace, they wouldn't
want such a king.

HISTORICAL AND BIBLICAL CUE: *Magi Ethnicity*

The three wise men were not Jews and were probably Arabs (Gentiles). Though Jesus did not deliberately seek out Gentiles during
his ministry, he did commission his disciples to make disciples

of all nations. He also spoke with Gentiles and used two Gentiles as examples of those blessed by prophets (Mark 7:24-30; Luke 4:26-27).

HISTORICAL CUE: *The Wise Men's Status and Character*

To make this journey and bring such gifts, these men would have been very rich. They were not snobbishly rich, however, for they humbly knelt down to a child, which makes you wonder at their insight. And they were not disillusioned by the less-than-wealthy circumstances of the family, but "overwhelmed with joy" (Matt. 2:10).

They also seemed to think outside whatever religion they practiced if they were willing to come to Judea. They must have been spiritually receptive for God to have chosen to speak to them through a dream (2:12). These seekers of wisdom were willing to bring enormous gifts and sacrifice their time and expense for this trip. Perhaps they were ready to do this because the celestial events surrounding Jesus' birth seemed to suggest that a powerful wisdom figure had entered the world, a figure they would want to meet and acknowledge.

Questions to Help You Enter the Story

Write a sentence or two in response to these this question:

1. How would it feel to take a long journey at great expense with limited knowledge of what I might find? How do I feel about taking such a risk? (Think of these men like Indiana Jones, crossing the world in pursuit of something they might not be successful at finding.)

Responding to the Story

Read the passage aloud again. Try to picture these men and imagine their facial expressions as they travel this long distance, interact with Herod, arrive at a peasant home, kneel before a baby, and present gifts to that baby.

- What do I as these men hear or see?
- What word, phrase, scene, or image emerges from the scripture and stays with me?
- What feelings do I imagine these men had?

Perhaps God is offering you an invitation in this passage to enlarge your understanding. In what way might that be? Sit quietly for a few minutes, pondering these questions:

- How is my life touched today by this passage?
- Is there some idea, feeling, or intention I need to embrace from it? If so, what?
- What might God be inviting me to be or know or understand or feel or even do?

Take a few minutes to respond to God about this in prayer.

- What do I most want to say to God about this experience in scripture?

Say whatever you need to say to God.

Sit in the quiet and consider:

- How did God (or God's actions) seem to me in this passage? What does this tell you about what God is like?

Spend a few minutes simply resting in God's presence. Finish by reciting the prayer of Ignatius on page 22.

EXPERIENCING THE JOURNEY TO SAFETY

Group Session
(Matthew 2:13-23)

Opening Ourselves *(10 minutes)*

Take a few deep breaths. Pray this opening prayer together:

> Let us release the cares of our day,
> and open our eyes to the wonder of God.
> With an attitude of empathy to people of another time,
> let us open our hearts and minds to God.
> Let us prepare to experience God's word to us
> through the presence of the Holy Spirit.

Entering the Story *(20 minutes)*

Read the session passage (Matt. 2:13-23) silently. The leader will then read the notes that follow the scripture text. Consider how they affect the story. Then close your eyes and listen as a group member reads the passage.

Matthew 2:13-23

¹³Now after they had left, an angel of the Lord appeared to Joseph in a dream and said, "Get up, take the child and his mother, and *flee to Egypt*, and remain there until I tell you; for Herod is about to search for the child, to destroy him."

¹⁴Then Joseph got up, took the child and his mother by night, and went to *Egypt*, ¹⁵and remained there until the death of Herod. This was to fulfill what had been spoken by the Lord through the prophet, "Out of Egypt I have called my son."

¹⁶When Herod saw that he had been tricked by the wise men, he was infuriated, and he sent and killed all the children in and around Bethlehem who were two years old or under, according to the time that he had learned from the wise men. ¹⁷Then was fulfilled what had been spoken through the prophet Jeremiah:

¹⁸ "A voice was heard in Ramah,

wailing and loud lamentation,

Rachel weeping for her children;

she refused to be consoled, because they are no more."

¹⁹When Herod died, *an angel of the Lord* suddenly appeared in a dream to Joseph in Egypt and said, ²⁰"Get up, take the child and his mother, and go to the land of Israel, for those who were seeking the child's life are dead."

Italicized Words & Phrases

flee to Egypt The distance from Bethlehem to Egypt is about 320 miles. If the family traveled twenty miles a day with a caravan, it would have taken about sixteen days. Mary and Joseph might have financed this journey with the wise men's gifts.

Egypt would have been a foreign culture. Joseph had to find work. Perhaps there was a Jewish colony there. Mary and Joseph may have wondered if they would ever return home.

angel of the Lord Once again, it isn't Gabriel who appears to Joseph but the angel of the Lord (Matt. 1:20, 24).

²¹Then Joseph got up, took the child and his mother, and went to the land of Israel. ²²But when he heard that Archelaus was ruling over **Judea** in place of his father Herod, he was afraid to go there. And after being warned in a dream, he went away to the district of Galilee. ²³There he made his home in a town called Nazareth, so that what had been spoken through the prophets might be fulfilled, "He will be called a Nazorean."

Judea It sounds like Joseph wished to settle in Judea, where perhaps Jesus' parentage would not make Mary such an outcast, but political pressures forced him back to Nazareth, where their secret was known.

CULTURAL CUE: *Mary and the Gentiles*

Living in a nation as an alien resident can be uncomfortable and often scary. Perhaps Mary was less scared living in the Gentile nation of Egypt because she had heard Simeon say that her son would be a "light for revelation to the Gentiles" (Luke 2:32) and because she had experienced the kindness of the Gentile wise men. Perhaps this also prepared her to hear Jesus later say that the Gentiles would receive God's blessing through Israelite prophets (the widow of Zarephath and Naaman [Luke 4:25-27]).

HISTORICAL CUE: *Herod's Wicked Character and Brutality*

Herod had one of his ten wives killed. He saw his sons as political rivals and had two of them killed. "Upon Herod's death the notables were to be executed so that there would be mourning in the land when the king died. Herod knew only too well that no one would weep for *him*. Fortunately, the order was not carried out."[1]

CULTURAL CUE FOR MODERN PEOPLE: *Why Study the Massacre of the Babies?*

It's thought that Matthew included this account about the horrible atrocities because he was presenting Jesus as the second Moses. Pharaoh had ordered the killing of all male Hebrew babies (Exod. 1:8-22), and Herod did the same.[2] Matthew wanted non-Jewish readers to understand that in their own eyes the Jews were still in slavery to their Roman oppressors, which is why they wanted the Messiah to be a military leader.

This story is important today. Wars in the Middle East have been frequent, as have been civil wars all over the globe. Two world wars ravaged Europe in the twentieth century. People have seen their friends and family killed by bullets and explosions.

"How do people retain their faith under such conditions? One answer is that they remember [that a] mindless, bloody atrocity took place at the birth of Jesus. . . . This story heighten[s] the reader's awareness of the willingness on the part of God to expose [God's] self to the total vulnerability which is at the heart of the incarnation. If the Gospel can flourish in a world that produces the slaughter of the innocents and the cross, the Gospel can flourish anywhere."[3]

Questions to Help You Enter the Story

Write a sentence or two in response to this question:

1. Mary and Joseph's life was full of hard tasks, including living down the infamy of a supposed illegitimate son and traveling to a faraway country to keep that child safe. It's important to see that difficulties are not eliminated when we cooperate with God, but that God walks with us. How might this truth be helpful to me today?

Responding to the Story *(15 minutes)*

As the leader reads the passage aloud, try to picture Mary and Joseph and imagine their facial expressions, or even put yourself in their places—traveling by night to Egypt.

- What do I (as Mary and Joseph or observing Mary and Joseph) hear or see?
- What word, phrase, scene, or image emerges from the scripture and stays with me?

- What feelings do I imagine Mary and Joseph had?

Perhaps God is offering you an invitation in this passage to enlarge your understanding. In what way might that be? Sit quietly for a few minutes, pondering these questions:

- How is my life touched today by this passage?
- Is there some idea, feeling, or intention I need to embrace from it? If so, what?
- What might God be inviting me to be or know or understand or feel or even do?

Take a few minutes to respond to God about this in prayer.

- What do I most want to say to God about this experience in scripture?

Say whatever you need to say to God.

Sit in the quiet and consider:

- How did God (or God's actions) seem to me in this passage? What does this tell me about what God is like?

Spend a few minutes simply resting in God's presence. Finish by reciting the prayer of Ignatius on page 22.

Group Sharing (10 minutes)

If you wish, share this: What do you think God might have been saying to you, inviting you to be or know or understand or feel or even do? If you don't wish to speak, listen attentively to other group members to see if their comments relate to you and also to see how God speaks to our sisters and brothers in Christ so differently from the way God speaks to us.

Closing Prayer *(5 minutes)*

> Grant us wisdom and courage this week:
> to trust you to provide ways out of danger;
> to weep with those who weep and be thankful for what we have;
> to taste and see your presence in new ways;
> to trust that you will do good and joyful things in our lives and
> in the world.

During the Week

Before going to bed or when you're doing a relatively simple chore
(for instance, taking out trash, washing dishes, locking doors before
retiring), reflect on this:

- Is there anything God might be leading me to do because of
  what came to me today in this passage?

  This must not be forced or contrived or according to the
  usual tapes that might play in your mind (for example, fix
  this person; make someone happy; correct people's thinking; strive a little harder). God may not be leading you to do
  anything; but if so, be open to what that might be.

BEFORE THE FIRST GROUP MEETING

Read the introduction to become familiar with the *Taste and See* approach to interacting with scripture. This method may be unfamiliar, and some people may need time to warm up to it. Others will love it immediately. If you have time, do the first meditation yourself.

Gather the following supplies before your group meets for the first time:

- Books for each participant
- Pens or pencils for participants
- Colored pens and drawing paper (optional)
- Large pillows for sitting on the floor (optional)

If possible, give participants a copy of the book before the initial meeting and ask them to read the introduction. If that is not possible, plan to mention items in the introduction that you think participants particularly need to know during your first session. Think about the previous experiences of group members. What do they need to know? The first session may require a little extra time for introductions and your opening comments.

SPECIAL EVENT: *THE NATIVITY STORY* (MOVIE)
2006, 101 min., Family Drama;
http://www.imdb.com/title/tt0762121/?ref_=sr_1

Watching *The Nativity Story* together will help members of the group imagine more easily the setting and characters they will meet in the coming weeks. The movie portrays well life in rural Nazareth; the trip to Bethlehem; the everyday lives, houses, and customs of people in that time; the reactions of Mary, Joseph, Joseph's friends, Mary's parents, the shepherds, the wise men, and Herod.

You may want to have dinner and watch the movie either before or after the first group meeting. Or you may decide to have a movie night some time after the study is underway. Be sure to fix popcorn!

When you watch the movie together, assign each member of the group to observe one of these aspects or characters depicted in the movie:

- Life in rural Nazareth (What were houses like? What were the sleeping arrangements? What surprised them?)
- The trip to Bethlehem and what travel was like
- The lifestyle, reactions, and feelings of Mary, Mary's parents, Zechariah, Elizabeth, Joseph, the shepherds, Elizabeth, Joseph's friends, Herod, the wise men.

After watching the movie, ask what people noticed about their assigned character or situation. The movie, of course, adapted some things (including the attitudes of the three wise men), but overall we come away knowing more than we did, and better able to imagine how life was lived and how events unfolded.

PATTERN FOR THE WEEKLY MEETINGS

Greet participants as they arrive. Once everyone is seated in a circle, invite them to introduce themselves if they do not know one another. At the first session, mention details from the introduction that you believe are particularly pertinent for the participants. In your opening remarks encourage participants in the group to be:

Open: You might say, "Don't try to control what you imagine. Be open to the Spirit's leading you into something new. Christmas is a time for wonder; this gathering is the place to wonder aloud and live in wonder."

Accepting: Some group members may say things you think are odd. Make a commitment now to avoid judging, giving advice, or criticizing, even if it's only in your mind (for example, *He is way off! She's never going to plug into this meditation!*). Try turning any negative self-talk into a prayer for the person or situation and then focus on the passage in front of you.

Opening Ourselves *(10 minutes)*

Invite participants to quiet themselves by sitting with arms and legs relaxed. Direct them to close their eyes and breathe in and out slowly a few times. Ask everyone to say the opening prayer together—slowly. (You may need to say that the prayer is more effective when recited slowly.) Suggest they sit quietly for another minute.

Entering the Story *(20 minutes)*

Reading the Scripture

- Ask participants to read the day's passage silently.
- Then read aloud the comments about particular words and phrases. (Please practice ahead any names that you might struggle to pronounce.)
- Instruct participants to close their eyes and listen as you read the passage aloud again.

Questions to Help Participants Enter the Story
See content specific for each session below.

Responding to the Story *(15 minutes)* See content specific for each session below.

Explain that God may be offering participants an invitation in this passage to know God better. In what way might that be? Encourage them to sit quietly for a few minutes; then, offer the following questions, allowing a few minutes after each one for participants to write their responses.

- How is your life touched today by this passage?
- Is there an idea, feeling, or intention you are called to embrace from the scripture? If so, what?

- What might God be inviting you to be or know or understand or feel or even do?

Invite those in the circle to respond to God in private, silent prayer for a few minutes.

Help group members by asking aloud:

What do you most want to say to God about this experience in scripture? You may wish to ask God questions (the answers to which may come to you through the group or later in the week.) You might want to write your prayers in this book. Writing prayers can help you focus and say more concretely what you're really thinking.

After a few minutes of time for prayer, invite group members to soak in the experience. You might say something like:

Sit in the quiet and consider: how did God seem to you in this passage? What was God like? Spend a few minutes simply resting in God's presence.

Group Sharing (10 minutes)

Invite group members to speak if they wish, asking questions related to the session (see below for each week's questions).

Remind participants that what they say aloud might be helpful to others. They may have found that their invitation from God feels incomplete or unresolved. Hearing what others say might help.

Reminder about Days 2–7

Before closing, point out the readings and exercises for Days 2 through 7. (If possible, do these yourself and call some participants during the week to see how they're doing with these or if they have any questions.)

Call group members' attention to the projects suggested at the end. Read them aloud and ask for additional ideas.

Closing Prayer (5 minutes)

Lead group members in saying the closing prayer together. Encourage them to say it slowly in a meditative way.

NOTES FOR EACH SUNDAY IN ADVENT

First Sunday of Advent
Zechariah's Surprise in the Temple (Luke 1:5-25)

Questions to Help Participants Enter the Story

Read the first question and ask people in the circle to offer their responses. Do the same with the other questions. People's responses will vary, which is to be expected. People will have different opinions (both positive and negative) on how Zechariah felt in these situations. Figuring out a "right" answer isn't the point. Entering the story—bringing the whole self into it—is the point. If group members need a little encouragement to verbalize their answers (often they do with the first question), here are some possible responses to the questions:

1. Zechariah may have felt honored and he may have been nervous.

2. Zechariah may have suspected many times that Elizabeth was pregnant when she was not. He may have been a little jaded. Or he may have been one of those matter-of-fact people who ask questions.

3. He may have been overwhelmed with feelings—even in tears—trying to express himself. Or he may have been frustrated that he couldn't talk. We can imagine him looking to Elizabeth to read his mind, as spouses sometimes expect each other to do.

Don't be concerned by group members who quickly attribute negative feelings to characters. First, they might be right! Second, they may be bringing their own feelings to the story. It works best to let that be. People need to get used to this kind of scripture experience and feel accepted within the group. You are free to offer positive suggestions as long as you don't appear to be correcting them.

Cues: Read each of the four Cues aloud to the group. Pause after each Cue, suggesting group members picture the scene or imagine the smell. (Biblical Cue: *An Angel's Appearance*; Historical Cue: *The Altar of Incense*; Sensory Cue: *Smell of Incense*; Picturing Cue: *Talking with Your Hands*).

Responding to the Story

Now explain that as you read the passage aloud to them again, they are invited to join the story. They can join the story in either one of these ways:

    1. Observe Zechariah. Watch him enter the sanctuary, converse with the angel, and then try to explain himself later with his hands.

    2. Put yourself in Zechariah's place and experience what happens to him.

Either way, consider the feelings and atmosphere the group has studied. Suggest participants close their eyes because this process is like making a movie in their mind. It can be fun. Participants may be surprised at what they imagine.

Pause after reading to allow group members time to enter the story fully.

Then ask, "What word, phrase, scene, or image emerges from the scripture and stays with you? What do you (as Zechariah or observing Zechariah) hear or see? What feelings do you imagine Zechariah had?"

Instruct participants to write their responses in the blank spaces provided. (At this time, they will not be sharing aloud.)

Group Sharing

- If you "joined the story," at what point did that happen?
- Did you see yourself as observing Zechariah or did you see yourself in Zechariah's place?
- What do you think God might have been saying to you, inviting you to be or know or understand or feel or even do?

Second Sunday of Advent
Gabriel Visits Mary (Luke 1:26-38)

Questions to Help Participants Enter the Story

Read the first question and ask people in the circle for their responses. Do the same with the suggestions. People's responses will vary, which is to be expected. Figuring out a "right" answer isn't the point. Entering the story—bringing the whole self into it—is the point. If group members need a little nudging to verbalize their answers, here are some "pump primers":

Did Mary's mouth become dry? Might she have wrapped her arms around herself in fear? What other reactions could she have had?

Give participants a minute to think. (Exercises 2 & 3 are designed to help group members *enter* the story in a right-brain way that encourages their creativity.) With number 3, you might want to lay some colored pens (or colored pieces of paper) in the center of the circle or table. Ask members to pick up the pen that best matches the color of their choice. People find it easier to pick a color when they see it in front of them. They often find it easier to share questions or insights if they can hold something in their hands.

3. Various choir cantatas have put the Magnificat to music. You might ask your choir director ahead of time if your church choir has performed any renditions of the Magnificat. If so, don't be too quick to name this example. Give people in the circle a chance to recall hearing the Magnificat sung and to come up with their own ideas.

This session offers no Cues, but many are offered throughout the coming week. If you'd like to use some in your group meeting, be ready to have a few people read the following from Week Two, Day 5:

BIBLICAL CUE: *"Magnificat" and the Great Inversion* (p. 53)
BIBLICAL AND HISTORICAL CUE: *What Mary Knew* (p. 53–54)
BIBLICAL AND HISTORICAL CUE: *What Mary Didn't Know (Future)* (p. 54)

Responding to the Story

Explain that as you read the passage aloud again, they are invited to join the story. They can join the story in either one of these ways:

1. Observe Mary. Watch her be stunned as an angel appears. Watch the perplexity on her face. Does she lick her lips before speaking because she is so surprised? What does she do with her hands or arms?

2. Put yourself in Mary's place. Experience the physical responses Mary might have had—perhaps her mouth becomes dry

or she stops breathing for a moment. How does your posture or position change as you say this sentence: "Here am I, the servant of the Lord; let it be with me according to your word"?

Pause after reading to allow group members time to enter the story fully. Then ask, What word, phrase, scene, or image emerges from the scripture and stays with you? What do you (as Mary or observing Mary) see or hear? What feelings do you imagine Mary had?

Invite participants to write their responses in the blanks provided. (At this time, they will not be sharing aloud.)

This Week's Project

Suggest to group members that they could include Mary's words in their prayer: "How can this be?" Or, "Here am I, the servant of the Lord; let it be with me according to your word."

When you call attention to the projects, ask participants if there are other ways of using music to pay attention to God and what God is doing in their lives.

Third Sunday of Advent
Joseph "the Just" and His Dreams (Matthew 1:18-25)

Entering the Story

Read each of the four Cues aloud to the group, pausing after each one to allow them to picture the scene or imagine the smell (one Cultural Cue about marriage customs, two Character Cues, and one Picturing Cue about Joseph).

Questions to Help Participants Enter the Story

If group members need encouragement to verbalize their answers, here are some suggestions:

1. Make sure you've read the character Cues about Joseph first in order to understand this question.

2. Try to think of an example from your life when you've chosen to set aside anger and be restorative (forgiving a relative, overlooking a co-worker's fault). Part of the nonviolence training many

civil rights workers received included responding with gracious-
ness when they were spit on or called names.

Be sure to include the second part of the question about the
feeling sensed when hearing such stories. This is important for the
time of scripture meditation.

Responding to the Story

Now explain that as you read the passage aloud to them again,
group members are invited to join the story in one of the following
ways:

1. Observe Joseph. Watch him discover the news about Mary's
pregnancy. How does he find out? Picture how he reacts in his
anguish and anger. Picture him reprocessing that anger into grace,
being restorative instead of accusative.

2. Put yourself in Joseph's place and experience what happens
to him. Feel within yourself what it's like to reprocess anger into
grace, to be restorative instead of accusative.

After reading, ask, "What word, phrase, scene, or image emerges
from the scripture and stays with you? What do you (as Joseph
or observing Joseph) hear or see? What feelings do you imagine
Joseph had?" Invite people to write down their responses in the
blanks provided. (At this time, they will not be sharing aloud.)

Group Sharing

Invite group members to speak if they wish, asking: "How did you
join the story? Did you see yourself as observing Joseph or perhaps
standing in Joseph's place? What do you think God might have
been saying to you, inviting you to be or know or understand or
feel or even do?"

This Week's Project

Ask participants if there are other ways of reprocessing anger into
grace that they might want to attempt. Remind them that we all
need God's empowerment to do this. Trying to do it on our own is
not a good idea. Consider committing to pray for one another in
this venture.

Fourth Sunday of Advent
Mary Gives Birth (Luke 2:1-7)

This session can work for a Christmas Eve or Christmas Day Meditation.

Many people have extra activities during Christmas week, so explain to participants that the group will go over "Experiencing the Birth of Christ" in this meeting and that throughout the week they can explore the situation more as time permits.

If you prefer, you can use other meditations for this time together. Here are the choices:

- Day 1: Mary Gives Birth (Luke 2:1-7)*
- Day 2: Joseph Arranges the Bethlehem Journey (Luke 2:1-7)*
- Day 3: A Family Receives Mary and Joseph (Luke 2:1-7)*
- Day 4: The Family That Kept Them: Thirty Years Later (Mark 10:13-16; Matthew 10:40-42)
- Day 5: The Shepherds' Mission (Luke 2:8-20)*
- Day 6: Simeon and Anna Celebrate (Luke 2:21-38)
- Day 7: Wise Men Come (Matthew 2:1-12)

  *Possible Christmas Eve or Christmas Day Meditation

If you are not meeting for a fifth week, suggest that group members use "Post–Advent: Experiencing the Journey to Safety" on Day 6 or Day 7 of this week.

Entering the Story

Read the Cultural and Historical Cues about setting. They present a very different understanding of the circumstances of Christ's birth. Participants may need a minute to let this soak in. Then read the Historical Cue about the journey.

Questions to Help Participants Enter the Story

Read the first question and ask people in the circle for their responses. Do the same with the other questions. If group members need encouragement to verbalize their answers, here are some suggestions:

1. Ask group members what difficult things they have encountered in their travel experiences.

2. You might be ready to read Luke 1:30-33, as suggested. Also ask those in the group who have had children how they felt when they looked upon their firstborn.

3. Mary no doubt was learning to trust God bit by bit, to be thankful for little things (even crowding in with another family in their main family room, giving birth among strangers).

Responding to the Story

As you read the passage aloud to them again, invite group members to join the story in one of these two ways:

1. Observe Mary and Joseph. Watch them move through their journey and then find refuge in a family's main room. How do they rely on each other?

2. Put yourself in Mary's place. Experience the probable fear of childbirth and of relying on strangers all around her.

3. Mary might have had a sense of cooperating with God's plan, or even partnering with God.

After the reading, ask, "What word, phrase, scene, or image emerges from the scripture and stays with you? What do you (as Mary or observing Mary) hear or see? What feelings do you imagine Mary had?"

Group Sharing

Invite group members to speak if they wish, asking: "How did you join the story? Did you see yourself as observing Mary or perhaps as standing in Mary's place? What do you think God might have been saying to you, inviting you to be or know or understand or feel or even do?"

Post–Advent Session
Experiencing the Journey to Safety (Matthew 2:13-23)

Entering the Story

Read first the Cultural Cue about how living among Gentiles might have affected Mary and how she responded to later events in her life. Then read the Historical Cue about Herod's brutal character, following closely with the Cultural Cue about why studying about the killing of the babies (Matt. 2:16-18) is important for people in our world.

Invite everyone to join the story in one of these two ways:

1. Observe Joseph or Mary. Feel with them the possible panic of rushing to save their baby's life, watching over him in Egypt, and being careful about when and where to return home.

2. Put yourself in Joseph's place or Mary's place and experience what is happening.

Questions to Help Participants Enter the Story

If group members need a little encouragement to verbalize their answers, here is a suggestion:

1. Participants will need a few minutes to think about this. If any group members are in transition or without a job and if you think it's wise, ask them what might be a next step in cooperating with God in their less-than-ideal circumstances.

Responding to the Story

After the reading, ask, "What word, phrase, scene, or image emerges from the scripture and stays with you? What do you (as Mary or Joseph) hear or see? What feelings do you imagine Joseph or Mary had?"

Direct people to write their responses in the blanks provided. (At this time, they will not be sharing aloud.)

Group Sharing

Invite group members to speak if they wish, asking:

- How did you join the story?
- Did you see yourself as observing Joseph (or Mary) or perhaps as standing in their place?
- What do you think God might have been saying to you, inviting you to be or know or understand or feel or even do?

Project: Think of someone you know who needs extra help, as Mary and Joseph no doubt did when they made their trip to Egypt. Maybe someone you know needs help moving or getting a driver's license or even learning a language.

A GUIDE FOR FAMILIES

This Advent guide makes use of "participative meditation," which is ideal for children whose imaginations are rich and well nurtured. Daydreamers and children who enjoy make-believe will excel at this. The story itself is ideal for a family because it's about a family. Even if your family is going through some struggles, this story is well-suited because the Holy Family did too.

DECIDING HOW OFTEN TO DO THE MEDITATIONS

There is a meditation for every day, but perhaps you will want to do this with your family only on Sundays or Wednesdays, for example. Week 4 includes special meditations for Christmas Eve and Christmas Day that you might want to use.

CHOOSING MEDITATIONS

Meditations with dialogue (which make them ideal to act out) include the following:

- Week One, Day 1: Zechariah's Surprise in the Temple (Days 2–4 are the same story from other points of view.)
- Week One, Day 5: John the Baptist Is Born
- Week Two, Day 1: Gabriel Visits Mary
- Week Two, Day 3: Mary Visits Elizabeth
- Week Three, Day 1: Joseph "the Just" and His Dreams (Days 2–5 are the same story from other points of view.)
- Week Two, Day 4: Elizabeth Responds to Mary's Visit
- Week Four, Day 5: The Shepherds' Mission
- Week Four, Day 6: Simeon and Anna Celebrate

You might want some sheets, pillowcases, and bathrobes for costumes. This doesn't have to be elaborate. Angels might want a flashlight to turn on when they "appear."

Meditations with activities that children might like include these:

- Week One, Day 6: Uses colored pens and color-coding of words.
- Week Two, Day 5: Children can make up a dance or do a dance.
- Week Four, Day 3: This meditation invites participants to consider being an inanimate object. Children might especially enjoy this. "I'm the manger! I held Jesus." Many children might like seeing themselves as the animals brought inside the house for the night. Scripture mentions none specifically, but if there was a feeding trough, then there were animals to eat out of it. Your children would have liberty to make up whatever kind of animal they want to be in the room. (This may be a good moment to involve their stuffed animals.) A parent might enjoy being the actual house—a safe structure to protect and provide for Jesus' little family.

Meditation about people coming to stay with others:

If you have people coming to stay with you (especially if your living space is small), you might prepare your children ahead of time with this meditation, which is about people coming to stay with others:

- Week Four, Day 3: A Family Receives Mary and Joseph (Luke 2:1-7)

Meditations that are particularly intergenerational (ideal if grandparents visit):

- Week One, Days 1–7: Experiencing the Blessing of Zechariah and Elizabeth
- Week Four, Day 6: Simeon and Anna Celebrate (Luke 2:21-38)

Meditation that exhausted parents might enjoy on their own:

- Post–Advent: Experiencing the Journey to Safety (Matt. 2:13-23)

Meditation to avoid with children:

- Post–Advent: Experiencing the Journey to Safety (Post–Advent includes the journey to Egypt but also the massacre of the infants).

Meditations about angels (to which children are sometimes drawn):

- Week One, Day 4: The Angel's Point of View (Luke 1:5-25)
- Week Two, Day 1: Gabriel Visits Mary (Luke 1:26-38)
- Week Two, Day 2: The Angel Speaks (Luke 1:13-17, 19-20, 28, 30-33, 35-37)
- Week Three, Day 1: Joseph "the Just" and His Dreams (Matt. 1:18-25)
- Week Four, Day 5: The Shepherds' Mission (Luke 2:8-20)

FOLLOWING THE GUIDE

Helping Children Settle Down and Settle In

- Opening Prayer: You might have a special opening prayer that will help you and your children to enter the quiet. Or there might be a calming slow song that helps, such as the Christmas carol "O Little Town of Bethlehem."
- Do the devotions in the same place each time. This will become a "thin place," a place where younger children easily connect with God. So your dinner table might not be best. Maybe sitting down by the Christmas tree, or sitting in front of your fireplace with a fire in it, or even everyone crowded around or on your bed in your bedroom. Going outside (in the Southern Hemisphere) might be possible, but also distracting.
- Lighting a candle at the beginning of your time together is a good idea. You may or may not have an Advent wreath, but a special Christmas candle would be good.

- If you like the idea of a special treat to eat or drink, try to stay away from something sugary that will make it difficult for children to stay engaged with you.
- Close by singing together "Silent Night."

READING FROM THE GUIDE

Have your children take turns reading such things as the italicized words and phrases, as well as the Cues below the text. But have a skilled reader read through the scripture text itself. Look ahead for words they might struggle to pronounce. If a child is going to read the scripture, let him or her practice earlier in the day if possible. This kind of meditation works best when words are clear and the reading is unhurried.

USING YOUR FAMILY CRÈCHE

If your family has a crèche, get it ready for the first meditation and use the figures needed for each scene. Do not get out the stable until it's needed. And be sure to hide the figure of baby Jesus somewhere special in your house until it can be used on Christmas Eve or Christmas Day! You can even invent some clues for finding it. Or you might let placing the Christ child in the crèche be a special reward for a child.

KEEPING HANDS OCCUPIED

If you have children who are easily distracted and seem to need to keep their hands busy, you might purchase a Christmas coloring book and have them color pictures as your family does the meditation together.

Or simply give the children something to hold. A miniature crèche tree ornament might be ideal.

DETAILS YOU CAN ADD

If your children have a Bible storybook with pictures, include that. Especially if you watched the movie *The Nativity Story*, you can print out images from the movie on the internet by going to Google Images and typing in: "the nativity story movie."

Week Four mentions a journey of eighty miles. Think of a place eighty miles from where you live that can serve as a meaningful comparison to the Holy Family's journey.

Children generally have better imaginations than adults. Enjoy that. They may come up with odd ideas. Please enter into their thoughts and affirm their contribution to the meditation experience.

NOTES

Introduction

1. John Mogabgab, "Editor's Introduction," *Weavings* 12, no. 1 (January–February, 1997), 2–3.
2. Richard J. Foster, *Celebration of Discipline: The Path to Spiritual Growth* (San Francisco: Harper & Row, 1988), 30–31.
3. *The Nativity Story*, directed by Catherine Hardwicke (2006, 101 min., family drama), http://www.imdb.com/title/tt0762121/?ref_=sr_1.

Week 1: Experiencing the Blessing of Zechariah and Elizabeth

1. Revised from the "Introduction to the Talk," Epiphany Ministry, Inc., www.epiphanyministry.org.
2. Alfred Edersheim, *The Life and Times of Jesus the Messiah* (Peabody, MA: Hendrickson, 1993), 95.
3. William Barclay, *The Gospel of Luke* (Philadelphia, PA: Westminster Press, 1956), 4.
4. Edersheim, *The Life and Times of Jesus the Messiah*, 97.
5. Barclay, *The Gospel of Luke*, 5.
6. James Orr, ed., *The International Standard Bible Encyclopedia*, vol. 3 (Grand Rapids, MI: Eerdmans,1939), see "incense."
7. "What Does Frankincense Smell Like?" Basenotes.net, accessed August 21, 2013, http://www.basenotes.net/t/290834/what-does-frankincense-smell-like.
8. David L. Fleming, S.J., *Draw Me Into Your Friendship: A Literal Translation and a Contemporary Reading of The Spiritual Exercises* (Saint Louis, MO: The Institute of Jesuit Resources, 1996), 177 (annotation 234).
9. N. T. Wright, *Following Jesus: Biblical Reflections on Discipleship* (Grand Rapids, MI: Eerdmans Publishing Co., 1994), 66.
10. Tom Wright, *Luke for Everyone* (Louisville, KY: Westminster John Knox Press, 2004), 18.

Week 2: Experiencing Mary's Preparation

1. John James Maclaren, *The International Standard Bible Encyclopedia*, vol. 3 (Grand Rapids, MI: Eerdmans, 1939), see "Jesus."
2. Norval Geldenhuys, *Commentary on the Gospel of Luke* (Grand Rapids, MI: Eerdmans Publishing Co., 1977), 82.
3. Dallas Willard, *The Divine Conspiracy: Rediscovering Our Hidden Life in God* (San Francisco, CA: HarperSanFrancisco, 1998), 120–21.
4. W. E. Vine, Merrill F. Unger, and William White Jr., *Vine's Expository Dictionary of Biblical Words* (Nashville, TN: Nelson, 1985), see "magnify."
5. Geldenhuys, *Commentary on the Gospel of Luke*, 85.
6. Willard, *The Divine Conspiracy*, 88–89.

Week 3: Experiencing Joseph's Challenge

1. Edersheim, *The Life and Times of Jesus the Messiah,* 106.
2. Kenneth E. Bailey, *Jesus Through Middle Eastern Eyes: Cultural Studies in the Gospels* (Downers Grove, IL: InterVarsity Press, 2008), 43.
3. Ibid., 45, re: "he became angry," citing Henry G. Liddell and R. Scott, *A Greek-English Lexicon,* rev. H. S. Jones and R. McKenzie (Oxford: Oxford University Press, 1966), 567.
4. Ibid., 46.
5. Richard A. Batey, *Jesus and the Forgotten City: New Light on Sepphoris and the Urban World of Jesus* (Grand Rapids, MI: Baker, 1991), 7, 14.
6. Ibid., 14.
7. Ibid., 71.
8. Ibid., 7, 15.
9. Ibid., 28.

Week 4: Experiencing the Birth of Christ

1. Bailey, *Jesus Through Middle Eastern Eyes,* 31.
2. Ibid., 29.
3. Ibid., 25–34.
4. "If the distance from Nazareth to Bethlehem is 80 miles how long would it have taken Mary and Joseph to walk the distance?," Answers, accessed July 18, 2013, http://wiki.answers.com/Q/If_the_distance_from_Nazareth_to_Bethlehem_is_80_miles_how_long_would_it_have_taken_Mary_and_Joseph_to_walk_the_distance.
5. "How far is Bethlehem from Jerusalem?," Answers, accessed August 2, 2013, http://wiki.answers.com/Q/How_far_is_Bethlehem_from_Jerusalem#page3.
6. Bailey, *Jesus Through Middle Eastern Eyes,* 25–34.
7. It doesn't appear that Jesus spoke these things in the Jerusalem or Bethlehem area, but family members might still have been present when Jesus said them. And he seemed to say the same things in several places (as most teachers do).
8. Trevor Hudson, *A Mile in My Shoes: Cultivating Compassion* (Nashville, TN: Upper Room Books, 2005), 57.
9. Bailey, *Jesus Through Middle Eastern Eyes,* 35.
10. Ibid.
11. Edersheim, *The Life and Times of Jesus the Messiah,* 132.
12. Geldenhuys, *Commentary on the Gospel of Luke,* 118.
13. Edersheim, *The Life and Times of Jesus the Messiah,* 137.
14. Tom Wright, *Matthew for Everyone: Part 1, Chapters 1–15* (Louisville, KY: Westminster John Knox Press, 2004), 10.
15. Bailey, *Jesus Through Middle Eastern Eyes,* 52.
16. Ibid., 56–57.

Post–Advent: Experiencing the Journey to Safety

1. Bailey, *Jesus Through Middle Eastern Eyes,* 57.
2. Ibid., 57–58.
3. Ibid., 58–59.

ABOUT THE AUTHOR

Jan Johnson is a writer, speaker, and spiritual director who holds degrees in Christian education and spirituality. She is the author of seventeen books, including *Enjoying the Presence of God, When the Soul Listens, Savoring God's Word*, and many magazine articles. She is also a frequent retreat and conference speaker. For more information about her writings and speaking engagements see www.jan johnson.org

CPSIA information can be obtained at www.ICGtesting.com
Printed in the USA
LVOW10s0547260915

455781LV00002B/2/P

9 780835 813549